THE ROYAL COURT THEA

T0247447

The Royal Court Theatre is t the leading force in world th.... . ... energetically cultivating writers – undiscovered, new, and established.

Through the writers the Royal Court is at the forefront of creating restless, alert, provocative theatre about now, inspiring audiences and influencing future writers. Through the writers the Royal Court strives to constantly reinvent the theatre ecology, creating theatre for everyone.

We invite and enable conversation and debate, allowing writers and their ideas to reach and resonate beyond the stage, and the public to share in the thinking.

Over 120,000 people visit the Royal Court in Sloane Square, London, each year and many thousands more see our work elsewhere through transfers to the West End and New York, national and international tours, residencies across London and site-specific work.

The Royal Court's extensive development activity encompasses a diverse range of writers and artists and includes an ongoing programme of writers' attachments, readings, workshops and playwriting groups. Twenty years of pioneering work around the world means the Royal Court has relationships with writers on every continent.

The Royal Court opens its doors to radical thinking and provocative discussion, and to the unheard voices and free thinkers that, through their writing, change our way of seeing.

Within the past sixty years, John Osborne, Arnold Wesker and Howard Brenton have all started their careers at the Court. Many others, including Caryl Churchill, Mark Ravenhill and Sarah Kane have followed. More recently, the theatre has found and fostered new writers such as Polly Stenham, Mike Bartlett, Bola Agbaje, Nick Payne and Rachel De-lahay and produced many iconic plays from Laura Wade's **Posh** to Bruce Norris' **Clybourne Park** and Jez Butterworth's **Jerusalem**. Royal Court plays from every decade are now performed on stage and taught in classrooms across the globe.

It is because of this commitment to the writer that we believe there is no more important theatre in the world than the Royal Court.

Supported using public funding by
ARTS COUNCIL ENGLAND

Robert Fox, Matthew Byam Shaw
for **Playful Productions** &
Royal Court Theatre Productions present
the Royal Court Theatre production of

HANGMEN

by MARTIN McDONAGH

Hangmen was first performed at the Royal Court Jerwood
Theatre Downstairs, Sloane Square, on Friday 11 September 2015
and at Wyndham's Theatre on Tuesday 1 December 2015

HANGMEN

by Martin McDonagh

At Wyndham's Theatre, the cast (in alphabetical order) was:

Hennessy **Josef Davies**
Clegg **James Dryden**
Mooney **Johnny Flynn**
Bill **Tony Hirst**
Pierrepoint **John Hodgkinson**
Shirley **Bronwyn James**
Harry **David Morrissey**
Syd **Andy Nyman**
Inspector Fry **Craig Parkinson**
Charlie **Ryan Pope**
Alice **Sally Rogers**
Guard **Mark Rose**
Arthur **Simon Rouse**

Writer **Martin McDonagh**
Director **Matthew Dunster**
Set and Costume Designer **Anna Fleischle**
Lighting Designer **Joshua Carr**
Sound Designer **Ian Dickinson for Autograph Sound**
Casting Director **Amy Ball**
Assistant Director **Roy Alexander Weise**
Production Manager **Jamie Maisey**
Costume Supervisor **Laura Hunt**
Fight Director **Kate Waters**
Dialect Coach **Zabarjad Salam**
Company Stage Manager **Heidi Lennard**
Deputy Stage Manager **Nina Scholar**
Assistant Stage Manager **Claire Baldwin**
Set built by **Scott Fleary & Cardiff Theatrical Services**

The Royal Court & Stage Management wish to thank the following for their help with this production: Bush Theatre, Diageo, Donmar Theatre, National Theatre, RSC.

Hangmen

by the same author from Faber

THE PILLOWMAN
IN BRUGES

published by Methuen

THE LEENANE TRILOGY
(*The Beauty Queen of Leenane,*
A Skull in Connemara, The Lonesome West)
THE CRIPPLE OF INISHMAAN
THE LIEUTENANT OF INISHMORE

MARTIN McDONAGH

Hangmen

FABER & FABER

First published in 2015
by Faber and Faber Limited
The Bindery, 51 Hatton Garden,
London ECIN 8HN

Reprinted with revisions 2015
First published in the US in 2016

Typeset by Country Setting, Kingsdown, Kent CT14 8ES
Printed in England by CPI Group (UK) Ltd, Croydon CRO 4YY

A CIP record for this book is available from the British Library

ISBN 978-0-571-32887-1

Hangmen was first performed in the Royal Court Jerwood Theatre Downstairs on 10 September 2015. The cast, in alphabetical order, was as follows:

Hennessy Josef Davies
Clegg James Dryden
Mooney Johnny Flynn
Bill Graeme Hawley
Pierrepoint John Hodgkinson
Inspector Fry Ralph Ineson
Shirley Bronwyn James
Harry David Morrissey
Charlie Ryan Pope
Alice Sally Rogers
Arthur Simon Rouse
Syd Reece Shearsmith

Director Matthew Dunster
Design Anna Fleischle
Lighting Joshua Carr
Sound Ian Dickinson

This production transferred to Wyndham's Theatre, London, on 1 December 2015, with the following changes of cast:

Bill Tony Hirst
Syd Andy Nyman
Inspector Fry Craig Parkinson

Characters

HANGMEN

Act One

SCENE ONE

Lights up on a prison cell in 1963. Table centre, at which sits James Hennessy, head on the table, terrified, two prison Guards sitting on either side of him, looking at each other. A clock starts chiming eight, and Hennessy raises his head, just as the cell door behind him swiftly opens and Harry Wade, in a suit and dicky-bow, and Syd Armfield, his assistant, enter, prompting Hennessy to jump to his feet, knocking his chair over. The Guards stand also. The Governor and Doctor stay outside, looking in.

Hennessy (*London accent*) Oh, you punctual bastards!

Harry It'll all go easier for ya, lad, if you just accept it and don't make a fuss.

Hennessy backs up over the table.

Hennessy Of course I'm going to make a fuss! I'm an innocent man! 'A fuss'!

Harry Get the strap on, Syd. Guards . . .

Hennessy What's the strap for? Who are them at the door?

Governor It's the governor and the doctor, James.

Hennessy Gawking at doors! This is *my* cell, get out!

He grabs on to his metal bedstead for dear life, curled up on the floor. The men try to prise him off throughout.

Harry Just go easy, lad!

Hennessy No I *won't* go easy! You go easy! You're hanging an innocent man! I never even *met* the girl! I've never even *been* to Norfolk!

Harry That's all just the whys and wherefores. That's nowt to do with me.

Hennessy Of course it's to do with you, you northern bastard!

Harry We'll have none of that 'northern' palaver neither!

Hennessy What's he saying? He can't even talk normal and he's hanging an innocent man! They could've at least sent Pierrepoint!

This strikes a raw nerve, stopping Harry in his tracks.

Harry I'm just as good as bloody Pierrepoint!

Hennessy Hung by a rubbish hangman, oh that's so me!

Syd He *is* just as good as Pierrepoint, Mr Hennessy.

Hennessy Well, he's shit so far!

Harry That's your bloody fault! Get his bloody arms!

They peel some fingers off the bedstead but don't get much further.

Hennessy It's only because I'm scared, isn't it? I'm not normally like this.

Harry And I've told ya, if you'd just relax, it'd be all the easier for ya.

Hennessy It won't be easier for me. I'll be dead.

Harry Everybody says you're a good lad.

Hennessy I *am* a good lad.

Harry We know you're a good lad.

Hennessy What are you fucking hanging me for then?!

Harry It's the courts that's hanging ya, not us.

Hennessy Well, I'm holding *you* and *you* personally responsible. Not you two – (*The Guards.*) You were nice. *You* two. I will come back to whatever northern shithole you live in and I will fucking haunt you.

Syd Well, that's not a nice thing to say, is it?

Harry Syd! You're just standing around having a chat like a bloody mouse!

Hennessy He's allowed to stand around having a chat like a bloody mouse if he wants to.

Syd No, but he's right, Mr Hennessy. If you'd've just tried to relax you could've been dead by now.

Hennessy Is he having a laugh? Is the mouse having a laugh? I'm getting hung by nincompoops!

  The struggling continues.

Syd 'Hanged'.

Hennessy Ay?

Syd You're getting 'hanged' by nincompoops.

Hennessy I've heard it all now! Correcting me English at a time like this!

Harry Let go of that bedstead now.

Hennessy I let go of this bedstead, I'm a dead man, so no, I won't let go of this bedstead, actually.

  Harry takes out a billyclub, looks at the Governor, from whom he gets no response, then goes over to the struggling group . . .

Harry He's right, of course.

> *. . . and thwacks Hennessy across the head. Groggy but still conscious, he slumps and releases his grip on the bed. The men outside the room let out an audible gasp.*

Governor Oh, I say . . .

Harry Shut it! Shut your bloody mouths. Stand him up.

> *The Guards stand Hennessy up and Syd quickly starts tying Hennessy's arms behind his back with the strap.*

(*To Syd.*) Having a nice chat, were we?

Syd I wasn't, Harry.

Harry 'You're getting hanged by bloody nincompoops'.

Hennessy Don't do it tight, I've got a bad wrist.

Harry You didn't have a bad wrist when you were clinging to that bedstead!

Hennessy I did!

Harry Do it tight!

> *Syd does so.*

And get ahold of him.

> *The Guards do so.*

And follow me.

> *A noose has appeared downstage of the cell. Hennessy sees it and his body sags. Harry walks towards it and the trapdoors it's hanging over, and the Guards and Syd walk Hennessy to it. Governor and Doctor quietly follow.*

Hennessy No no no no no, it's not fair. I never even met the girl, Mr Wade. I've never had a problem with the ladies. Ask anybody. Why would I do a nasty thing like that?

Harry It's nowt to do with me, is it, lad?

Hennessy But I've never even *been* to Norfolk. Or anywhere in East Anglia.

Harry slips the hood and noose over Hennessy's head, as Syd swiftly straps his legs.

What's that, a hood? I don't want a hood. Can I not have the hood? I promise I'll go quietly if I don't have to have the hood . . .

Almost before the words are out, Syd rolls away from the strapped legs, Harry pulls a lever to one side, the trap beneath Hennessy's feet falls and his body drops below floor level, the rope pulling taut, breaking his neck, hanging him there, out of sight. Harry and Syd step up to the edge of the trapdoors, looking down on the hanging body, followed by the others.

Harry Where's doctor?

Doctor Here, sir.

Harry Well go down and bloody check on him, lad.

Doctor Right!

The Doctor heads down, out of sight, to check the body.

Harry Have *somebody* do their bloody job properly today. (*To the Guards.*) Where'd they get you two? Window at fucking Debenhams?! (*To Syd.*) And as for you!

Syd What were I supposed to do, Harry? He were clinging on to that b- b- bedstead . . .

Harry 'Bedstead'. Here comes the stutter . . .

Syd B- b- bedstead . . .

Harry 'Bedstead'.

Syd For dear life.

Harry Finished, have ya? 'Bedstead'? (*To Governor.*) And we'll have none of this going down int' bloody report, neither!

Governor Oh yes, no. Of course.

Harry He went to his death protesting his innocence. End of story. Saves his blushes, saves these lads' blushes, saves 'Bedsteads' blushes. Are we right?

Governor We're right, yes.

Harry We're right, good. (*Pause.*) Albert bloody Pierrepoint.

The Doctor comes back up, taking stethoscope off.

Doctor Yes, he's dead. Quite dead.

Harry Course he's quite dead. What else would he be? (*Pause.*) Now where's our bloody breakfast? I, for one, am fucking starved.

Blackout.

SCENE TWO

A large, old-fashioned pub on the outskirts of Oldham circa 1965, two years after the previous scene. Harry behind bar in his usual dicky-bow, pulling pints with his wife, Alice. Five men at the bar; the three 'cronies' – Bill, Charlie, and Arthur (the oldest and a touch deaf) – Clegg, a local journalist, and a plainclothes policeman of Harry's age, Inspector Fry. All are from the north of England and when they get going, they speak at quite a pace.

Clegg But you must have a comment, Harry.

Fry Must he?

Harry I do have a comment, lad. 'No comment'.

The cronies laugh.

Charlie That were a good one, Harry. 'No comment'.

Arthur What were it?

Charlie Newspaper lad says, 'But you must have a comment, Harry.' Harry says 'I do have a comment. No comment.'

Arthur That were a good one! He just said same thing first lad said.

Clegg Oh Harry, I've driven all the way up from Manchester.

Harry You'll be driving all the way down to Manchester an' all. Commentless!

Laughter from all.

Arthur What did he say?

Charlie He said 'Piss off back to Manchester' . . .

Harry I didn't say 'Piss off', Charlie . . .

Charlie 'Commentless'!

Arthur What-less?

Charlie 'Commentless'!

Arthur That were good!

Fry Do you want us to arrest him, Harry lad? Or just give him a bloody hiding?

Clegg Arrest me for what, Inspector?

Fry For being under age in a public bar, for a start off. How old are ya, twelve?

Laughter.

Harry Five, more like!

Much more laughter.

Charlie Inspector says, 'How old are ya, twelve?' Harry says, 'Five more like!'

Arthur Ha ha, younger, I get it.

Clegg Come on, Harry, it's not every day they abolish hanging, is it? You must have summat to say.

Harry It's not, lad, you're right. And I know that's why half o' you bastards are in here today . . .

Alice Language, Harry!

Harry And I *do* have my opinions on this abolition business. How could I not, like? Same as I've had a variety of opinions over the years, on a variety of subjects . . .

Bill He's had a variety of opinions on subjects over the years, I've heard 'em . . .

Harry But one thing . . . You *haven't* heard 'em, Bill, that's what I'm saying, cos one thing I've always prided myself on, for right or for wrong, I'm not saying I'm a special man, but one thing I've prided myself on is that, on the subject of hanging, I've always chosen to keep me own counsel. I've always chosen not to say a public word on this very private matter, and why have I chosen to do that, you may ask?

Arthur Why?

Harry For the past twenty-five year now I've been a servant of the Crown in the capacity of hangman. 'A

18

what of the Crown?' did you say? 'A *spokesman* for the Crown'?

Charlie No. A *servant* of the Crown!

Harry A *servant* of the Crown. And when was the last time you heard a servant making speeches . . .?

Bill *Russia* . . .

Harry (*same time*) *Never* . . . 'Russia'? You'd be shot if you made a speech in Russia, what are ya talking about, Bill?

Bill No, I were thinking in the olden days.

Harry Well, it were even worse in the olden days, stop talking daft, Bill. Bill's talking daft again! A *servant* of the Crown. I let the other people make the speeches; the politicians, the ministers, the . . . devil's advocates. Sometimes the police inspectors when they've sobered up enough, oops, sorry, Inspector Fry, I didn't see ya there!

Laughter.

Fry Apology accepted, hic!

Charlie 'Sobered up', he were saying, and then the police inspector says 'Hic'!

Arthur Aye. I don't get it, but I don't know the man.

Charlie You *do* know the man . . .

Harry Me? I keep me own counsel. A day *will* come when fellas finally see some sense and ask me my opinion . . .

A young stranger called Mooney comes in, takes his overcoat off, sits at a side table. Harry keeps an eye on him.

. . . But until that bright day comes, I will be quite content to keep me own counsel, as I see fit, and leave the jibber-jabber to the riff-raff, the riff-raff being you sorry lot. Now who wants a bloody pint?!

All except Clegg call for a pint. Harry and Alice pour and serve among a general hubbub.

Clegg But that day *has* come, Harry. We *have* seen sense. I *am* asking your opinion.

Harry (*with an edge*) Aye, and I already told ya, lad . . .

Fry He already told ya, lad . . .

Harry (*calling out to Mooney*) And there's no table service!

Mooney slowly gets up and ambles over.

Alice Ease up, love. Lad's only just took his coat off . . .

Harry Well, I know the type, don't I? Sitting down.

Alice (*to Mooney*) Pint is it, love?

Mooney (*London accent*) Pint, yes, and a small bag of peanuts.

Alice We've only the one size. I'll get you them.

Alice gets the nuts and starts pouring his pint.

Harry London, are ya?

Mooney Round that way.

Harry Well, you either are or ya aren't.

Mooney Exactly.

Bill (*to Clegg*) I've got a quote for ya, lad.

Clegg Yeah, what's that then?

Bill 'Hanging's too good for 'em.' Cos it is, int it?

Clegg (*sarcastic*) Oh right, aye. Thanks.

Bill The country thinks that, the people think that. It's only the politicians disagree, which is the crossroads at which we find ourselves today. In a right jam. Int that right, Harry?

Harry Int what right?

Bill That hanging's too good for 'em.

Harry Didn't I just do a big bloody speech about keeping me own counsel, Bill? I wouldn't be keeping me own bloody counsel if I made a comment on that, would I? Ya daft pillock! Why do I even try?

Charlie It's true, Harry! You shouldn't even try!

Bill No, I were just saying. I were just agreeing, like. Hanging's too good for 'em, int it?

Harry stops and glares at him. Fry smiles to himself.

Harry Have yourself another pint, Bill. And try to keep up!

Bill I'll have another pint, Alice!

Laughter from the men as the slight tension is diffused.

Religion and politics, int it? They say you should never something something something.

Alice (*to Mooney*) There's your pint and your peanuts, love. That's a shilling.

Mooney That's very good value.

He pays and a muttered hubbub continues as Harry and Mooney look at each other on his way back to table, where he sits with his pint, back to the bar, opening his paper and nuts, reading.

Alice So what were up with her then, George? Phyllis Keane, you were saying earlier.

21

Fry What were up with her?

Alice That you'd have to do summat that drastic.

Fry I'll tell you what were up with her. Every car number plate that passed, she'd have to read it out, out loud. *Every* car, mind. That's a lot of cars in Burnley. Every broken paving stone she passed she'd have to . . . either step *on* it or *not* step on it, I can't remember which, but again, Burnley, you'd be hopping all day. And what were t'other one?

Alice That's a famous one though, int it, paving stones? I wouldn't go by that.

Harry Oh give over, Alice.

Alice What?

Harry You're always defending daft uns.

Alice I'm not.

Fry Bodies of water! She'd have to walk clockwise around bodies of water. Lakes or bridges, like. Clockwise.

Harry Burnley, you'd be alright.

Fry No, anti-clockwise. She'd have to keep them on her left.

Alice Yeah, but we all have things like that, don't we, George? Quirks. It's no call to put a poor girl in a mental home.

Harry *I* don't have things like that!

Fry *I* don't have things like that!

Harry *I* don't have quirks! *I* don't have to read out every car number plate that passes! *I* don't do that, *you* don't do that!

Alice Sometimes I'll read one out in me head, if they're a funny one.

Harry Well, how is reading something out in your head, reading something out out loud?!

Alice No, he's right there!

Harry On top of the bloody paving stones! On top of the bloody clockwise!

Fry Anti-clockwise.

Harry Anti-clockwise.

Alice It's no call to put a girl in a home is all I'm saying. At fifteen, like.

Harry Who the hell are we talking about, any road?

Fry Phyllis Keane.

Harry Who?!

Alice She's a school friend of our Shirley's.

Harry Oh. Does our Shirley know?

Fry No, she were only sent down this after.

Harry Let's not tell her till bedtime, Alice. It's any excuse to mope with our Shirley.

Alice Teens, int it? It's the music, for me.

Harry Int the music. It's the sitting around on your fat arse all day, mooning . . .

Bill (*same time*) Reading.

Harry What?

Bill 'Sitting around on your fat arse all day, reading.'

Harry Not 'reading'. Mooning.

Bill Oh.

Harry You stay out of it any road.

Mooney (*calling out*) Could I have another pint, please?
I'll come over once it's poured.

*Harry glares at the back of his head, but Alice pours
the pint.*

Alice Don't mind him, love. He just don't know the
ropes, does he?

Harry There's ropes and there's ropes, though, int there?

Fry Well, that were my afternoon, any road. Driving
nutters about. Then I thought I'd pop o'er here to *your*
nutters, and make sure you didn't get any shite from
newspaper reporters or under-age drinkers . . . Oh sorry,
Clegg, are you still here, lad?

Laughter from cronies. Mooney picks up his pint.

Mooney Thanks. I'm only halfway through the nuts so
I won't get any more of them.

Alice Alright, love.

Mooney I'm slow with nuts.

Charlie Another two here, Harry, please.

*As Mooney returns to his table he whispers something
in Clegg's ear, which Clegg is a little startled by . . .*

Clegg What was that?

Mooney You heard.

*. . . and continues back to his table, leaving Clegg
somewhat perplexed, as down the stairs behind the
bar comes Shirley, Harry and Alice's fifteen-year-old
daughter.*

Harry Speak of the devil!

Shirley The devil? Me? How, Dad?

Fry Howdo, Shirley.

Shirley Howdo, Inspector Fry. Lads.

Harry Well, are you helping pull pints or are you just going to stand there like a cloud?

Shirley Oh, aye.

She starts helping behind the bar.

Stand there like a what?

Harry Like a clown.

Shirley Oh. I thought you said 'cloud'.

Clegg I think I'll go now then, Mr Wade.

Harry Alright, lad. I suppose your mam'll be wondering where you are.

Laughter from cronies.

Charlie His mam!

Arthur He said his mam and he's not even that young, he's probably got his own place to stay, like a flat!

Clegg No. The paper said I were to speak to Albert Pierrepoint too, see if he's got –

The pub suddenly goes silent and Harry stops what he's doing to stare at him. Mooney quietly closes his paper.

– owt to say about this abolition business. (*Pause.*) Him being, y'know . . . the Number One hangman all them years. (*Pause.*) And that.

Harry Oh aye?

Clegg Aye. Over at his pub. What's it called again?

Mooney 'Help the Poor Struggler'. It's a very good pub, actually.

Harry Pierrepoint's pub's Failsworth. You'd've passed Pierrepoint's pub ont' way. Why didn't you pop in on road o'er?

Clegg Why?

Harry Aye! Why?!

Clegg Well . . . it's obvious, isn't it?

Harry (*cold*) If it were obvious, lad, I wouldn't be asking, would I?

Shirley Dad . . .

Mooney He does have a point. Why didn't you just ask at Pierrepoint's pub ont' road o'er'?

Clegg (*stalling*) Well . . . I wanted a quote from *the* hangman, didn't I? The hangman that was still called upon at hanging's dying days. The one whose opinion *matters*. Not from some bloody has-been who quit his post ten years since. (*Pause.*) Y'know?

Mooney smiles and returns to his paper, as Harry finds a freshly poured pint in his hand.

Harry (*to Clegg, cheerily*) Was this your pint, lad?

Charlie No, it were . . .

Clegg I were just going, Harry . . .

Charlie It were mine . . .

Harry Stay for your pint, lad, it's poured now.

Alice It's on the house.

Harry It int on the house but it's poured now, so you're having it. Right. Now, I don't mind talking to ya, but

26

we'll be doing it upstairs, away from the prying ears of these bloody jackdaws . . .

Groans from the nosey cronies.

Bill Oh Harry!

Harry And I'll be talking to ya off the record because, as I believe I said to ya before, I like to keep me own counsel. Now step this way . . .

Clegg But there's no point talking, Harry, if it's going to be off the record.

Harry Don't push your . . .

Clegg Pierrepoint wasn't going to be off the record . . .

Harry Don't push your fucking luck, alright? Don't push your luck. (*To Mooney*) And what are you smirking at?!

Mooney There's a photo in the paper of a funny-looking black chap.

Harry (*pause*) Upstairs if you want to chat.

He heads upstairs, Clegg following, taking his pen and notebook back out.

Alice But it's a pigsty upstairs, Harry . . .

Harry Well, whose bloody fault is that?!

They're gone, the cronies a little miffed.

Charlie Oh . . .

Arthur Is Harry gone?

Alice Looks like it, don't it?

Arthur How long's he going to be gone for?

Alice Well, I don't know, do I? This is a circus, not a . . . This is a pub, not a three-ring bloody circus!

Arthur (*pause*) Will he be a while?

Alice sighs and heads towards the pub's front doors, taking her cigarettes out.

Shirley Where are you going, Mam?

Alice Fag.

Shirley I can't serve on me own!

Alice Yeah ya can. It'll do you good. Take you out of yourself.

She's gone. Shirley shyly collects glasses, etc., tries to make herself small.

Arthur I were going to have another pint, but if hangman's gone off I might go. I don't even like the pints here, but they've a hangman.

Fry This is the hangman's daughter, Arthur. Shirley.

Arthur I know. I know that from before. Where's this tother hangman's pub?

Charlie Failsworth.

Arthur Failsworth? Failsworth's miles. Well, I don't know whether to wait for the hangman to come back or to go. I only came for t' hangman.

Fry Have another pint, Arthur! Jesus!

Arthur I will!

Mooney finishes his pint and goes up to the bar.

Mooney I'll have the same again, please, Miss.

Shirley Oh. Which one were it? I weren't here.

Mooney I dunno. Doesn't really matter, does it, they're all the same, really, aren't they?

Fry They're not.

Mooney They're all the same up north, aren't they?

Shirley I don't drink, so I don't know.

Mooney Good for you. Shirley, is it? Why don't you do a lucky dip, Shirley, and I'll have that one?

Shirley Really? Shall I? Like a lucky dip? Alright . . .

She starts doing a count under her breath, like the children's picking game . . .

You are *not* it . . .

She continues the count, ruling the first one out.

Mooney Could take quite some time.

Fry Have I met you before, I'm thinking?

Mooney Me? How am I supposed to know? I do get about.

Shirley (*counting*) *You* are *not* it.

She starts the count again, ruling out the first two . . .

You are *not* it! It's Guinness!

She goes to pour a Guinness.

Mooney Oh, actually, I don't like Guinness. I meant any of the other ones.

Shirley Oh . . .

Mooney I thought you understood. I'll just have a pint of mild.

She smiles and pours a mild.

It's quite specific, isn't it, Guinness?

Shirley Yes, it's quite Irish, isn't it?

Mooney It is, isn't it. I'd say nothing gets past you.

Fry You look more of a Babycham man, from where I'm standing.

Mooney I look more of a what man?

Fry A Babycham man. A man drinks Babycham.

Shirley Leave off, Inspector.

Mooney I don't know what that is, a Babycham man.

Shirley It's like a fizzy wine what's got a reindeer on it. Or a normal deer, I can't remember.

Mooney I wouldn't know anything about it. I'm not from around these parts, you see.

Fry Babycham's not from around these parts, is it? It's a southern drink.

Mooney Is it?

Fry It is, aye.

Mooney You seem to know a lot about it.

Fry I don't. You do.

Mooney We've established I don't.

Fry You going to have any more peanuts with your mild, or have you had enough peanuts?

Mooney I've still got a couple left from before.

Fry Have ya?

Mooney Yeah. I saved a couple for emergencies.

Shirley For peanut emergencies?

Mooney Yeah. In case I get trapped in a lift with a gorilla.

Shirley laughs.

Or a policeman.

Fry Alright . . .

Shirley Does that happen to you often?

Mooney Only when I'm in Wales.

Shirley You want to stop going to Wales then.

Mooney I know, but I keep getting drawn back. It's the gorillas, isn't it?

Fry You wanna watch yourself, lad. We're not all friendly up north.

Shirley I am!

Mooney She is.

Fry She's not everyone, is she?

Mooney She could be if she tried harder.

Shirley That doesn't make any sense!

Mooney (*beat*) Oh really. And how's your friend Phyllis?

Shirley Phyllis? Do you know Phyllis?

Mooney Phyllis? No. Phyllis Keane? No.

Shirley You do. You know her name.

Fry Alright, lad. Very good.

Mooney Did you like that? Did you like how I made that turn, Officer?

Fry We'll leave it at that then, shall we?

Mooney No more of this Babycham business then. I know only too well what Babycham is. I know all of its connotations. Alright?

Mooney drinks his pint in one.

Shirley, do you know of anyone renting rooms out around here?

Shirley Our mam used to rent rooms out but then she stopped.

Mooney Why, what happened?

Shirley Nothing happened. I don't think. She just stopped. Maybe people were getting too nosey.

Fry That were it.

Mooney Nosey about what?

Shirley Well, me dad.

Mooney What about your dad?

Shirley looks to Fry for help.

Shirley Well, nowt.

Mooney Is he famous?

Shirley Not famous, no.

Charlie He is.

Arthur He's a famous hangman.

Mooney Well, I'll be alright then cos luckily I don't care about that sort of thing. I've never had that kind of prurience. I'll go have a chat with your mum, shall I? She's outside having a fag, isn't she?

Shirley Aye, she's having a fag outside.

Mooney Yeah, I just said that.

He goes, taking his paper and coat on the way.

Shirley But . . . *do* you know Phyllis?

Mooney (*dreamily*) Do I know Phyllis?

He exits.

Shirley Well, does he?

Arthur Who were the chatty fella, Shirley? The new Babycham man?

Shirley No, just some fella. I think!

Shirley pulls a Babycham bottle from the bar and looks at its label.

It *is* a reindeer, int it. He's right cute! (*Puts it away.*) I couldn't work out if he *did* know Phyllis or if he *didn't* know Phyllis.

Fry Phyllis were taken away today, Shirley. To a home. Happen he may've just overheard summat.

Shirley Phyllis was?

Fry Aye.

Shirley Why?

Fry I don't know, love.

Charlie You do know.

Shirley (*pause*) What kind of a home?

Fry I don't know.

Charlie You said a mental home earlier.

Fry *I* didn't say that. Her mam said that.

Shirley Our mam knows? Why didn't she tell us?

Bill Because your dad said you'd just go moping if they told ya.

Fry Christ . . .

Shirley *My* dad said?

Charlie Aye.

Arthur Aye what? I missed all this.

Charlie Shirley's dad said Shirley was moody and she'd just go around moping about this Phyllis Keane being put in a mental home was why no one said owt to her about it.

Arthur Oh. Girl talk!

Shirley (*quietly*) It's Phyllis Keane's dad what wants putting in a home. Not Phyllis.

Alice comes back in and picks up some glasses as she heads back behind the bar.

Alice Here's news, love! We might be taking in a lodger if his references pan out and your dad don't start mithering about house guests again.

Shirley (*moodily*) Oh aye, that's nice.

Alice What have you gone all mopey for? You were fine five minute since.

Shirley I haven't gone all mopey!

Clegg returns hurriedly from upstairs, putting his notepad away happily.

Clegg If that's a man who keeps his own counsel I'd love to meet a fella as never stops yakking.

Fry Got your quote, did ya?

Clegg (*knocking back drink*) Got me front page, mate. I'll be seeing ya.

Arthur See ya, young lad!

Clegg exits.

Who were that?

Charlie Newspaper lad.

Arthur Everybody's new!

Harry comes back down, full of himself.

Fry You were in with him a while, Harry.

Arthur We almost went home!

Harry I just needed to set the lad right on a few matters, didn't I? But he were right about one thing, though. It *is* a momentous day.

Alice Well I just hope you didn't lose the run of yourself, that's all . . .

Harry Oh just shut your bloody cakehole, woman, and charge these men's glasses, for Christ's sake. It's a momentous bloody day, int it? 'Lose the run of meself' . . . *(To Shirley.)* And what have you gone all mopey for?! You were fine five minute since!

Shirley storms off upstairs, tearfully.

Oh, bloody teens!

All now have pints, Harry included, Alice has a gin.

Gentlemen? A toast . . . The End . . . of Hanging.

Bill Well I'm not toasting that!

Harry You bloody will, Bill, if you want to keep supping in this bar!

Bill begrudgingly raises his glass.

All The End of Hanging!

They drink.

Harry I won't know what to do with meself!

They all laugh, but in the slight pause afterwards, Harry really does wonder what he'll do with himself.

Blackout.

Lights up on Harry and Clegg at front of stage, facing out front, a large newspaper photograph of Harry in bowler hat and dicky-bow on a scrim behind them, a stylised approximation of their interview.

Clegg So your friend Bill said, 'Hanging's too good for them,' Harry, . . .

Harry Bill's a customer, not a friend, and he's a daft customer at that. Hanging int too good for them, hanging's just right for them. There are some fellas out there who are bad uns, and if the courts say they've got to go they've got to go, but if they've got to go they've got to go by the quickest, the most dignified and the least painful way of going as possible. That, in my book, in most normals people's books, is hanging.

Clegg But how do you know, Harry? You haven't seen any of the other methods of execution, the electric chair, or the firing squad . . .

Harry Of course I bloody haven't, I'm from Lancashire, not Arkansas! 'The electric bloody chair.' I'm told when that goes wrong they come out sizzling like a bloody steak! No thank you! I'll have my executions without the need for fried onions if it's all the same to you. Yank claptrap!

Clegg Guillotine's quick, I'd wager.

Harry Guillotine's quick but guillotine's messy and French. Who'd go for that in Durham? No one. And who's going to clean up mess after? Heads bouncing round. *I'm* not going to clean it up after. Warders? They've enough on their plate, the poor sods.

Clegg So how many men have you hanged, Harry? Give me a rough estimate.

Harry I pride myself on never having deigned that question with an answer, Derek, and I shall stick to that deigning.

Clegg More than a hundred?

Harry Loads more.

Clegg More than a thousand?

Harry Don't be daft, this int China!

Clegg More than Pierrepoint?

Harry See, now you're trying to come the smartarse again, aren't ya, like before. Everybody knows Albert Pierrepoint did shitloads, but Pierrepoint did a shitload of Germans both during and after the war, so there should be a bit of an asterisk against some of his numbers at the very least. Albert were doing fifteen to twenty of those bastards a day, after the trials got going proper, and I'd've been happy to lend a hand, I would, but Pierrepoint had that entire scene sewn up, didn't he? He wouldn't let us get a look in edgeways and I'd've been happy to hang some Germans, I'd've been chuffed. I never liked them *before* the war, let alone *during*. The accent alone . . .

Clegg Why weren't you asked, Harry?

Harry I *were* asked the first time around, around Nuremburg, but I were still a part-time bookie then and it coincided with Grand National Week so, y'know . . .? I probably should've gone. I fobbed them off, said the wife was poorly, and she probably was, she always is, but they never called me back again after that, cos they're like that, they say nowt, but they hold things agin ya. I regret not going, I'd've liked to see a bit of Germany. All I'm saying though is, all them Nazis Pierrepoint did, all them bastards as ran the camps and

whatnot, I hold my hand up to him, I do. Good riddance
to the lot of them, the swine. All I'm saying is, they
shouldn't be allowed to go on his final score. Cos
hanging Germans en masse, well, it int a hard job, is it?
They do what they're told, don't they, they follow orders.
'Stand o'er there, under that noose.' 'Alright, Sergeant
Pierrepoint, owt else I can do for ya?' 'Nay lad, you're
right.' Thunk! So if you subtracted Albert's Nazis from
his normals, I'm not saying I'd win, but we'd definitely be
running neck and neck. If you'll pardon the expression.

Clegg It would be great for the paper if you gave me a
number, Harry. How many have you done all in all?

Harry I won't, lad. I've no comment.

Clegg The low two hundreds?

Harry Higher.

Clegg The low three hundreds?

Harry You were close enough first time, the *mid* two
hundreds, but I'll leave it at that, the mid two hundreds.
(*Pause.*) Two hundred and thirty-three. Sans a single
German.

Clegg Nice. Although they say Pierrepoint's runs into the
six hundreds.

Harry Who says? Pierrepoint's wife? Bollocks. *And* his
hair smelled.

Clegg And whose hair smelled?

Harry Pierrepoint's hair smelled. They don't mention
that in the papers, do they?

Clegg What did it smell of?

Harry When I were in a mood I'd say it smelled of
death, but it were probably just stale Brylcreem.

Clegg (*writing*) 'Stale Brylcreem . . .' And, one final thing, Harry. The miscarriages of justice that've occurred over the last ten years . . .

Harry Oh, here we go, you had to spoil it . . .

Clegg The ones that have swayed public opinion against hanging . . .

Harry Says you.

Clegg Were most of those carried out by you or by Pierrepoint?

Harry Oh. (*Pause.*) Pierrepoint. Definitely. I think.

Clegg Derek Bentley?

Harry The retard? Pierrepoint.

Clegg Timothy Evans?

Harry The Christie lad? That was Pierrepoint, although I assisted, so technically that's 2–1.

Clegg Ruth Ellis?

Harry Pierrepoint. 3–1. Pierrepoint never seemed to mind hanging women. I did. I mean, you'd do it, it were the job, but it'd leave a nasty taste in your mouth weeks after.

Clegg James Hennessy?

Harry Hennessy weren't a miscarriage of justice. I read up on Hennessy after. He were your classic woman-hating psychopath and I don't usually like commenting on the people I've hanged but in his case, sod him, bad rubbish, good riddance.

Clegg He died protesting his innocence, they say.

Harry He were just scared, lad. They're all just scared. Some show it, some don't. Mostly what I remember about Hennessy, he were very anti-northern, and I don't like that. It's prejudice.

Clegg There was another woman attacked in Norfolk last year, out Lowestoft way, the police are saying, bore a lot of the hallmarks of the Hennessy killing . . .

Harry There'll always be women attacked, lad. It's just the nature of men, int it? In Lowestoft especially, there's nowt else to do. You soon get bored of miniature golf!

Clegg So are you saying, then, that the death penalty never worked as a deterrent, Harry?

Harry Aha! Good one, ya little bastard. I'll tell ya this, any road, Hennessy never killed anybody after I got ahold of him. You can be sure of that.

Clegg Maybe he never killed anybody before you got ahold of him?

Harry And maybe we'll never know. Boo hoo. Another pint, lad?

Blackout.

SCENE FOUR

The pub, the following morning. Alice, in her dressing gown, unlocks and opens the front door, takes in the milk and the local newspaper, locks the door again and finds Harry's interview in the paper.

Alice Oh Harry . . .

She pours herself a gin as she continues reading.

I wasn't poorly around Nuremburg. I'm never poorly. You just wanted a piss up at Aintree with your mates. (*Reads. Tuts.*) They're our friends now, the Germans.

(*Reads.*) 'Lowestoft'. You don't know the first thing about Lowestoft. You don't know the first thing about nowt. (*Reads.*) And there weren't nowt wrong with Albert Pierrepoint's hair. He had nice hair. (*Quietly.*) Unlike yours. (*Drinks some gin.*) He's lost run of himself. I knew he would.

She folds the paper away as Shirley comes down.

Morning, our Shirley. (*Pause.*) I says 'Morning, our Shirley'!

Shirley Morning. Do mental homes have visiting hours?

Alice You can get mental-home-visiting out of your head for a start-off. I thought we heard the end of that Phyllis Keane palaver last night. I wouldn't let you go to *Burnley* on your own, let alone to a Burnley mental home.

Shirley She'll be all on her own with nutters.

Alice Oh aye. Sounds like me at opening time. Your dad's lost run of himself in paper. I knew he would. Won't hurt business, though, the likes of folk round here. Probably help business. They'd pay to watch a car crash if you could slow one down. They're just morbid. (*Pause.*) Two hundred and thirty-three. (*Pause.*) I'd stop you reading it if I didn't think you'd get ahold of it one way or t' other.

Shirley I don't want to read it, do I? I don't care.

Alice You'd care if it were Elvis Presley.

Shirley Wouldn't be Elvis Presley though, would it? Elvis Presley don't hang folk. Elvis Presley don't say people are moody and mopey behind their backs neither.

Alice Oh, we're not still on that, are we? He didn't say it behind your back, did he? You were standing right there. (*Quietly.*) In a mood.

41

Shirley I weren't in a mood. I'm never in a mood. You're always saying I'm in a mood. I'm just shy.

Alice Well, how is shy going to help you in life?

Shirley Well, it's not, is it, but I can't help it, can I?

Alice But shy . . . It's just the same as mopey, shy.

Shirley It's not the same as mopey. I smile. Mopey don't smile.

Alice It's just the same as boring, shy.

Shirley It isn't. I'm not boring. It just depends who's on the outside, looking in.

Alice Well, the people who are on the outside looking in around here . . .

Shirley Think I'm boring.

Alice No. Think you're a mope.

Shirley Well, maybe I think they're boring too.

Alice Well . . . maybe you'd be right.

Shirley Maybe I think you and dad are boring an' all.

Alice Don't be stupid. We're not boring. I run a pub and he's chief hangman. That int boring, that's interesting. Meals on wheels for the depressed, that's boring.

Shirley He were chief hangman yesterday. He int nowt today.

Alice He'll be chief hangman for a long time yet, you mark my words. In his own mind if nowhere else.

She observes Shirley for a few moments.

Listen, love, I know you've started taking an interest in fellas . . .

Shirley I haven't! Where's this come from?!

Alice All those music magazines you go moping over . . .
gawking over . . .

Shirley I don't mope, Mam!

Alice Boys aren't interested in mopey girls, or shy girls.
Or, if they are, then they're interested in mopey girls who
are drop-dead gorgeous, so they can put the mopey to
one side.

Shirley But I'm pretty on the inside, Mam!

Alice But you're not though, love! You're moody on the
inside and mopey on the outside. No boy wants that
combo. So think on.

Shirley Think on, what? A frontal lobotomy?

Alice That wouldn't work with you. You're too pig-
headed. No, maybe there's some after-school courses you
could take on, might take you out of yourself. Archery
or badminton. Something as would get you moving.
I think you're pretty on the inside, love, you're my little
girl, aren't ya? I think you're pretty on the *outside* too.
It's just others.

There's a tuneful knock on the pub's front door.

Oh who the bloody hell's that when we're having a
heart-to-heart? And me in me blooming dressing gown.
You get it, Shirley.

Shirley I'm not getting it. I'm shy. I don't get doors.

Alice You get doors when it suits.

Shirley It's in the shy charter. No door-getting. I'll mope
over here.

*The knock sounds again. Alice goes over and gets it,
covering herself up.*

43

Alice Oh hello, Mr Mooney. What are you doing here at this hour?

Mooney Well, I've come with my references and for that chat you wanted.

Alice Oh. But it's nine in the morning, love.

Mooney I know. Shows I'm keen, don't it? (*To Shirley.*) Hello there again from yesterday.

Shirley Hello there again.

Alice I thought we'd said the afternoon.

Mooney No, no. (*Pause.*) The afternoon wasn't mentioned. No, no. That's why I'm here now.

Alice Oh. I'd best go put something on then. Can't be chatting in me dressing gown, can I?

Mooney Well that's up to you, isn't it?

Alice Well . . . I can't. Shirley, will you get Mr Mooney a cup of tea if he wants while I pop upstairs. These are your references, are they?

Mooney Yes. They're all typed up perfect, look. Margins. You've got to, these days.

Alice Right, I'll bring them with me, have a peruse.

Mooney You'll bring them with you, will you?

Alice Yes.

Mooney You'll bring them with you upstairs, will you?

Alice Yes, if that's alright?

Mooney (*beat*) That's alright.

> *He gives them to her and she goes upstairs. Shirley puts the kettle on, smiles shyly. Mooney sits at the same table as yesterday.*

This is the table I was sitting at yesterday.

Shirley Yes. That's like your regular table now, isn't it?

Mooney moves to a different table.

Mooney It was. I've changed it. I like to shake things up. (*Pause.*) Keeps people on their toes, y'know?

Shirley Aye.

She pours the tea.

Milk and sugar, Mr Mooney?

Mooney *Peter.*

Shirley Milk and sugar, Peter?

Mooney No, I don't drink tea.

Shirley Oh.

Mooney No, your mum said I did, but I don't.

Shirley Oh . . .

Mooney You can have it if you want. I don't want it.

Shirley Well . . . I shall! And two sugars. Even though I shouldn't!

Silence a while. An embarrassed laugh from Shirley. More silence. She drinks some tea.

Mooney You're quite a shy girl, aren't you?

Shirley splutters out her tea.

Shirley What?!

Mooney Yes. I noticed that yesterday.

Shirley Well . . . I'm not as shy as some.

Mooney I can't hear you.

Shirley (*louder*) I said I'm not as shy as some.

Mooney Oh no? Like who?

Shirley Eh?

Mooney Like who aren't you as shy as?

Shirley Well . . . I don't know. All sorts.

Mooney Footballers?

Shirley Well, I'm shyer than footballers.

Mooney (*pause*) Nuns?

Shirley Nuns? (*Pause.*) I'd say some nuns are shyer than me. It depends on the nun, don't it!

Mooney Yes. The new nuns, just starting out, who don't know the ropes . . .

Shirley Yes, I'd say I'm not as shy as them nuns. Not half as shy!

Mooney (*pause*) Paraplegics?

Shirley I suppose it depends on if they were shy before they had their accident, doesn't it?

Mooney Yes, good point. Or if they were born that way and there was no accident. (*Pause.*) Some paraplegics can be right grumpy pigs. (*Pause.*) But then you would be. (*Pause.*) I don't know what I'd do if I was a paraplegic. (*Pause.*) Nothing, probably.

Shirley (*pause*) I'd say, if it were a *mute* paraplegic, I reckon I'd be less shy than him. Or her, if he were a girl mute paraplegic.

Mooney You're quite funny.

Shirley Am I? I'm not.

Mooney You are. I noticed that yesterday.

Shirley Did ya?

Mooney I suppose certain people round here, it just goes over their heads, your sense of humour.

Shirley I don't know about that! But maybe.

Mooney Oh, there's no maybe about it. It's just hard to come across as funny, isn't it, when you're surrounded by stupid thicks. I've always found, anyway. That said, although I appreciate a good sense of humour, I don't actually come across as funny myself . . .

Shirley *I* think you . . .

Mooney Shush. Even when I try to be funny, I come across more as menacing. Which is ridiculous, because I'm nice. But no, as hard as I try, *menacing*. And then the label sticks, doesn't it?

Shirley *I* think you come across as funny.

Mooney Do you? Not menacing? Not even with that shush I just gave you?

Shirley No. I think you come across as funny, but different.

Mooney Funny but different. Like Groucho Marx.

Shirley I don't know. I don't really know the old ones.

Mooney He was a Jew, but you couldn't really tell.

Shirley Was he the one with the moustache?

Mooney Yes.

Shirley Right. I know who you mean.

Mooney (*pause*) How old are you anyway?

Shirley Fifteen.

Mooney (*pause*) A lovely age.

Shirley It int.

Mooney Int it?

Shirley Everybody just keeps having a go at ya, and you're not allowed to do nowt.

Mooney Well, don't let them have a go at you then.

Shirley (*tearfully*) I know, but it's hard, int it, when they're all bigger.

> *She starts to cry a little. Mooney goes over and gives her a pat, which she welcomes. There's nothing creepy about it, in fact he's almost too cold. He goes back to his seat.*

I hope my mam lets you have the room. That's all I can say. You'd liven the place up. (*Takes out a tissue.*) Bloody nose is full of bloody . . . mucus now, from that crying.

Mooney Well, yeah, I don't need to know that.

Shirley But d'you know what I couldn't fathom out from yesterday?

Mooney No, what couldn't you fathom out from yesterday?

Shirley *Do* you know Phyllis Keane or *don't* ya?

Mooney Phyllis Keane? I don't, actually, no.

Shirley I thought not, cos I was sure she'd've mentioned ya.

Mooney No. I just thought they all seemed to be ganging up on you, so I didn't want you to feel so all alone.

Shirley They *were* all ganging up on me. The bastards.

Mooney (*pause*) Poor Phyllis.

48

Shirley I know. I'm sitting here crying even though nothing's really wrong and she's sitting in a mental home for reading car number plates out loud. It int fair, is it?

Mooney Why don't you go visit her? Cheer yourselves up.

Shirley I were thinking that, but I don't know how it works with the visiting hours and it's miles.

Mooney I'll drive ya.

Shirley Will ya? Would ya?

Mooney If you want. I don't care, do I?

Shirley (*pause*) But what if they're closed?

Mooney If they're closed they're closed. We can't do anything about it if they're closed. Well, we could pop to the seaside then try again later, I suppose. It depends on if it's sunny, doesn't it?

Shirley I don't know.

Mooney Suit yourself.

Shirley (*pause*) What kind of car have ya?

Mooney A Morris Minor. It's a banger, but it'll get you there. I gave it a turtle wax last week. I didn't have to, I just felt like it. Where's her mental home, Burnley?

Shirley Burnley, aye, it's not too far. It's far on a bus, but not far in a car.

Mooney Where's the nearest seaside to Burnley?

Shirley I don't know. Formby?

Mooney Do you have a swimsuit?

Shirley Eh?

Mooney Do you have a swimsuit?

Shirley (*pause*) Maybe.

Mooney What colour is it?

Shirley Yellow. With dots.

Mooney Yes, that would go well with your hair colouring.

Shirley Would it?

Mooney Yes. Does the sand go in your swimsuit, when you're sitting on the sand down at Formby, or Walton-on-the-Naze, or wherever?

Shirley The sand?

Mooney Yes.

Shirley (*pause*) I usually get a deckchair.

Mooney Do you? A deckchair?

Shirley Aye! They're only cheap!

Mooney I see. (*Pause.*) But the times when you *don't* get a deckchair, and you're sitting on the sand, does the sand go in your swimsuit then? In those places I was getting at before.

Shirley Well, I've never been to Walton-on-the-Naze. Or anywhere in Norfolk. Is it Norfolk?

Mooney Maybe.

Shirley Aye. I've never been.

Mooney How comes? Too Fancy O'Reilly?

Shirley Well, no, you go wherever your mam and dad take you, don't you, when you're fifteen.

Mooney I don't. I choose not to.

Shirley But you're not fifteen, Peter.

Mooney Aren't I? No, of course I'm not, am I? I was just trying to confuse you. (*Pause.*) *I've* been to Walton-on-the-Naze. I've been there many times. (*Pause.*) I don't even know what a Naze is, but I've been to Walton on it.

Shirley (*pause*) I think it's like a curved headland. Although I'm not sure.

Mooney Well, I don't even know what a headland is. I suppose that makes me dense.

Shirley No. If you didn't know what a curve was, that'd make you dense.

Mooney (*pause*) There's that sense of humour again, I pointed out before. (*Pause.*) A curve, it's just a thing that goes like this, isn't it . . .

He makes the shape of a curve in the air with his finger. She nods. Uncomfortable pause.

Your mum takes a lot of time to put her clothes on, doesn't she?

Shirley Aye.

Mooney Oh, does she?

Shirley What?

Mooney Take a lot of time to put her clothes on.

Shirley I don't know. I suppose.

Mooney (*pause*) Well, if you still want to see Phyllis, and the seaside or whatever, why don't you meet me under the clock at the train station at eleven, after I'm finished chatting with your mum?

Shirley I don't know, Mr Mooney. I don't know.

Mooney (*pause*) Phyllis'll be missing you by now. All those mad people, screaming their heads off.

Shirley I just don't know.

Mooney No?

Shirley I'm shy about these types of things.

Mooney Oh.

Shirley I've never been out with a boy before.

Mooney Well, it's not going out, is it? I was just going to take you to a mental home. It's hardly tea at the Ritz. Although I think I put you off a bit, didn't I, with my talk about the sand and your swimsuit, I can see that now. I can see how that might've sounded strange. I'm just interested in sand. (*Pause.*) That's where I'll be, anyway. The clock at the train station.

Shirley (*pause*) Alright. I'll have a think about it.

Mooney I just get flustered sometimes because I'm shy.

Shirley Are ya?

Mooney nods.

What time at the train station, did you say?

Mooney Eleven.

She smiles, nods, and goes upstairs. He sits there a while, staring into space.

'Shy'. Fuck me.

After a moment, Alice comes down, dressed up nice.

Alice I took ages, didn't I? Oh, is Shirley not with you?

Mooney She *was* with me, but then she left.

Alice Of course she did. Well, I can see you didn't pinch anything from behind bar, so that's a good sign for a start off! Now, I couldn't get through on the phone numbers you gave me, that's why I took so long, they just rang and rang, but I shall try them again later.

Mooney You rang them already, did you?

Alice I did, but as I say, they just rang and rang.

Mooney That was very speedy of you.

Alice Like as not they hadn't got into the office as yet.

Mooney That was very thorough. That was very sneaky, phoning up my references behind my back while I'm standing down here waiting like a lemon.

Alice But I'm allowed to phone your references, Mr Mooney. That's what they're for, references.

Mooney Yes, I understand that. But the timing was very sneaky, wasn't it?

Alice Well, I've got to say, I'm a bit perplexed.

Mooney Perplexed, are you?

Alice Yes.

Mooney Well, *be* perplexed!

Alice Well, I am!

Mooney Yeah, no, I don't want the room now. No, I don't even want to look at it. Even if you apologised. Phoning my references?! Your husband's killed two hundred fucking people! Where's *his* fucking references?!

He walks out, slamming the door. Alice sits there dumbfounded. Harry comes downstairs, half dressed.

Harry What the bloody hell were that?!

Alice I don't know! I'm shaken, Harry. I'm quite shaken. It was the lodger fella. He were standing there normal, then he just flipped.

Harry Lodgers? They're just animals, Alice, I've told you that before. Oh, is that paper?

He opens the paper up to the page he's on, looks at the big photo of him in bowler hat and dicky-bow.

Alice Why shouldn't I've phoned his references? It's what you do with references, int it? Phone 'em.

Harry (*distracted*) Aye.

Alice Maybe they do it different down south, but I can't see how. (*Pause.*) I only wanted to find out if he were as lovely as he seemed. (*Pause.*) I'm not sure if I'd've wanted him around Shirley now, a fella who could turn that quick. (*Pause.*) I'm perplexed, honestly I am.

Harry Hardly matters what interview says when photograph's that good, does it? But I like the way it's reading so far. Albert bloody Pierrepoint. Take that, ya bastard!

Blackout.

SCENE FIVE

The pub, later that afternoon. Harry tidying glasses as Bill, Charlie, Arthur and Inspector Fry chat at the bar.

Bill All *I'm* saying is, from a *non-biased* point of view, that were the greatest interview I've seen printed in that newspaper in my entire life.

Charlie In any newspaper!

Bill In any newspaper!

Harry I'm too close to it, aren't I, so I can't say.

Arthur I'm just at start of it cos I left me glasses at home, so don't spoil it by saying owt.

Fry There's nothing to spoil, Arthur. It's an interview, lad.

54

Harry That said, it gets better as it goes on, so you don't want to spoil it in that sense, y'know?

Charlie My favourite bit was bit about the Germans.

Bill Mine too!

Charlie Cos they *are* swine. *Always* were. My other favourite bit was your saying your Alice was sick so's you could go t' Grand National!

Bill My favourite bit were bit about hanging's too good for 'em, because it is!

Harry Yeah, I never said that, Bill. I said you said that, and I said it were stupid . . .

Bill And my other favourite bit were . . . D'you know, I never realised Albert Pierrepoint were such a cock!

Harry Cock's too harsh, Bill. Cock's too harsh. Arrogant. Tight-fisted. Curmudgeonly. Mean. But cock's too harsh.

Charlie What were your favourite bit, Inspector?

Bill He liked photo! Cos he's queer!

Harry Are you starting again, Bill?! Do you want to be shown outside?

Bill No.

Harry Then calm bloody down, and ease up on your drinking! It's only two in the bloody afternoon, lad!

Bill Sorry, Harry.

Harry (*pause*) Inspector. The floor is yours.

Fry What floor?

Harry What was *your* favourite bit? 'What floor?'

Fry Oh. Aye. No . . . as I say, you made your case well about, y'know, hanging being the most dignified of the . . .

Charlie Well, it is!

Bill It is!

Charlie It's pure dignified!

Harry There speaks . . . *In vino veritas*, from the lads!

Charlie Other ones, you come out like fried steak!

Harry You do, though!

Arthur I'm just on the fried steak bit now. It's good. Onions!

Fry But, overall, I just think you went a bit far, that's all.

Uncomfortable silence from all.

I mean, nobody needs to know numbers, do they? Or what was said int' death cell, or who were scared or who weren't scared. Some things ought to remain, I don't know, sacrosanct or summat.

Harry (*pause*) Well . . . I agree, don't I? It says in black and white I refused to deign to give him a number, doesn't it, at start?

Fry It does, at start, aye. Later it says two hundred and thirty-three.

Bill (*pause*) He wormed it out of you, didn't he, Harry?

Harry He wormed it out of me, that's right.

Bill The bastard!

Harry The bastard.

Fry I know. That's what lad's like.

Harry I know!

Fry That's why I said you shouldn't've talked to him int' first place.

56

Harry By, you're in a funny mood today, George. Just because *you're* not int' paper, were it?

Fry No. I don't like being int' paper.

Harry You do!

Fry I don't. It interferes with me job.

Harry Oh aye, and what time are you due into office today, Inspector?

Fry looks at his watch . . . and at the pint in his hand. He smiles, and Bill and Charlie laugh.

Fry Aha!

Harry His job! Eh!

Laughter from all, except Arthur.

Arthur What were it?

Charlie Harry says to Inspector, 'What time are ya due int office?' Inspector looks at his watch, he looks at his pint, he says . . . (*Tuts.*)

Arthur Aye. He drinks too much.

Charlie No. No, not 'He drinks too much', Arthur. More he's in here when he should be in work, like, that's all.

Arthur Ohh . . . I see.

Alice comes down, worried.

Alice Is there still no sign?

Harry No sign of what?

Alice No sign of our Shirley!

Harry I'd've told you if there'd been a bloody sign, wouldn't I?! I'd've shouted up 'Mope's back!'

Alice But she's never missed her dinnertime without telling us and I've done us a blancmange for after.

57

Harry Oh, she's probably just gone off moping somewheres. Found somewheres new to mope.

Alice Aye, she was a bit mopey this morning, wasn't she? Hello, lads.

The lads say hello as the front door creaks open and all heads turn to see Syd Armfield, Harry's former assistant, enter.

Syd Howdo!

Alice Here, that's your Syd, int it? Hello, Syd!

Syd Hello, Alice! Hello, Harry!

Harry He int *my* Syd . . .

Alice We haven't seen you in a coon's age, Syd.

Syd No, well, I'm mostly Halifax, aren't I? Hello, Inspector, lads.

Arthur Hello, lad.

Fry Where do I know Syd from? I'm terrible with faces. Bad trait in a policeman!

Syd No, people often . . . forget me face and that. No, I used to be an assistant of Harry's, back in the day . . .

The cronies are audibly more welcoming now . . .

Charlie *and* **Bill** Oh-h . . .

Syd His main assistant, really.

Harry No, you were right first time.

Charlie Pull up a chair, lad. Have yourself a pint.

Syd I'll have a half, so.

Alice I'll be upstairs, Harry, in case she calls.

Harry In case who calls . . .? Oh! Aye, aye.

Alice heads off upstairs.

Alice Nice to see you, Syd.

Syd You too, Alice.

Harry Wish I could say same.

Syd Oh. Why?

Harry snorts.

Arthur Aye, why?

Harry I shall keep me own counsel, as they say. Here's your half, lad. That's fourpence.

Syd pays as he takes his drink.

Syd Cheers. Good health, lads.

Charlie *and* **Bill** Aye, cheers. / Cheers.

Syd (*drinks*) Em, Harry, would it be possible to have a quiet word at some point . . .?

Harry I'm run off me feet, lad, you can see that! It's a pub, not a sewing circle! And what drags you all the way down from Halifax the one day I'm all over the newspapers, I wonder?

Syd The newspapers? Are ya? Which ones?

Harry Well, the *Gazette*!

Bill He is!

Charlie It's there!

Syd I haven't seen. Is it good?

Charlie (*same time*) It's great!

Bill (*same time*) It's brilliant!

Arthur (*same time*) I haven't finished it, but it's good so far.

Harry glances at the silent Fry, who just sips his pint.

Syd I must have a read of it after.

Harry If you like, although you can buy your own. Aye, Syd used be me assistant in the hanging trade, a few year back this is, but after a series of mistakes and minor misdemeanours what finally broke the camel's back, what finally caused me to have to let him go . . .

Syd Oh you don't have to, do you, Harry . . .?

Harry What finally put the kibosh on his assistant hanging career were his commenting upon, and his laughing at, the size of the private parts of a Manchester gangster we were cleaning up the body of after hanging him at Winson Green. Dignity and the basics of human respect were all we owed that lad at that sad time and did he get them? Off this lad? Did he bugger!

Syd Aye, and I knew it were wrong, Harry, and I apologised at the time, didn't I? It's just . . . and I'll say it again . . . it were enormous!

Charlie laughs out loud.

Arthur What were it?

Charlie Enormous!

Harry (*cutting them off sharply*) Int funny! Int funny at all!

Bill Int funny!

Harry Weren't then! Int now!

Syd But I didn't mean nothing by it, did I? I were just surprised by it.

Fry tries to stifle a laugh but can't quite.

Harry (*to Fry*) I expect more from you. (*Pause.*) On the subject of 'sacrosanct'.

Syd Weren't just long, it were wide . . .

Harry Have you finished?! (*Pause.*) 'It were wide.'
(*Pause.*) Years later, in an incident not entirely unrelated,
he were sent to Leeds Prison six month for the sale and
distribution of obscene magazines, weren't ya, Syd?

Syd It *were* unrelated! How were it related?! Them were
fannies, not cocks! I wouldn't distribute cocks! And they
were legal in Holland, them fannies! H- h- how were I
supposed to know?!

Harry Any road, that's the nature of the character of
me assistant Syd Armfield. Now, a quiet word, were it,
S- S- Syd?

Fry You go too far, Harry . . .

Harry I say 'S- S- Syd' cos he used to have a stutter
when he got stressed, didn't ya, S- S- Syd? You probably
still do.

Syd I don't know if I should tell ya now. I- I- I came
here to help ya. I thought that cock were water under a
bridge . . .

Harry comes out and ushers Syd to a quiet table.

Harry Calm down, lad, I were only having a laugh,
weren't I? Now what were it you were after?

Syd I'm not after nowt, am I? I came here to be nice,
didn't I? I didn't expect to have cocks thrown in me face.

Harry Calm down you about cocks! Come o'er here. Sit
down. And sip your half. Now what's on your mind?

Syd Well, it's this Hennessy business, int it?

Harry Hennessy business? What Hennessy business?

Syd Well, I- I- I . . .

Harry Oh here we go . . .

Syd I didn't think about it much at the time. I didn't think about it for a year after, the Hennessy hanging. I mean, it were a bit of a balls-up but it weren't *botched*, were it?

Harry It weren't near botched. It were instant death once we got him ont' trap. Folk forget that.

Syd But, I suppose, him having so much time to talk . . . to *protest*, I suppose, and to threaten us, y'know? Well, it went beyond the usual frightened, didn't it?

Harry No. It went exactly the normal frightened.

Syd In the years after, I thought, I couldn't help but think . . . he weren't frightened. He were innocent.

Harry Oh, here we go! Is this what this is? All the way from Halifax for this shite?

Syd And if he were innocent, we hung an innocent man, didn't we?

Harry '*Hanged*' an innocent man! '*Hanged*' an innocent man! And, no, we didn't hang an innocent man. I went and read every court report on the bloody case after, just to set me mind at rest. He were guilty as sin, that perve.

Syd He were a car thief, Harry. He never had anything funny with women his entire life . . .

Harry Well, you've got to start somewhere, don't ya?

Syd But he were up in Blackpool the night before, a tart signed an affidavit –

Harry 'A tart signed an affidavit', by heck . . .

Syd – saying he were with her all night and he treated her nice. Why would he drive three hundred miles next day to do that to a girl on a beach in Norfolk?

Harry Let's reopen case, we've evidence from a tart!

I don't know why he did it, do I? Maybe he fancied a nice drive?! Perverts like driving too, y'know?

Syd A lass were attacked in Lowestoft a year to the day that we hanged him . . .

Harry Oh 'Lowestoft', Jesus . . .

Syd A year *to the day*, Harry. She survived. She described the fella who did it.

Harry Oh aye?

Syd She said he looked just like this man I were visited by this Saturday past. I don't know how he found me, but he said he had some photos he'd took, he asked me if I wanted to buy 'em. I thought he were messing with us, y'know, that he'd heard about me conviction or summat but they were photos of the girl on that beach in Lowestoft. And they weren't nice photos, neither, Harry.

Harry Bought them then, did ya?

Syd No. I wouldn't buy photos like that. (*Pause.*) He knew who I were, Harry. He knew I'd helped hang Hennessy. Then he said he were heading out Oldham way, he had some business out here. It was only last night I thought 'Oldham way', he might mean 'Harry Wade's way'. You haven't had anybody funny hanging about the pub the last couple of days, have ya?

Harry (*pause*) What did he look like, this fella?

Syd (*describes Mooney*) Well, he were a skinny fella, short blond hair. London accent, I think, and well enough dressed but a sort of a *menacing* look to him. Not a *hard* look, but a *menacing* look. In his eyes, like. (*Pause.*) I'm probably putting two and two together and coming up with five, aren't I? But I thought best be ont' safe side, cos it's second anniversary of Hennessy hanging today, int it?

Harry Is it? Don't time fly?

Syd Aye. I suppose. I dunno.

Bill (*calling out*) There's three of us parched over here, Harry lad . . .!

Harry Shut your bloody noise you, ya pisshead, I'll be over in a bloody minute, won't I?!

Bill I were only saying . . .

Harry Well, stop saying, Bill! Stop saying! (*Pause.*) Do you want another half, Syd?

    They get up to return to the bar.

Syd I won't, I'll be heading off, Harry. I only came up to tell you so's you'd, y'know, keep an extra eye on your Alice and your Shirley, like. Y'know? But I'm sure everything'll be fine.

    Harry starts pulling pints again, worried.

Harry Same again all round, is it, lads?

Charlie Aye.

Arthur Aye.

Bill I'll have a whisky, Harry.

Harry You'll have a pint like everyone else and stop your nonsense.

Bill I'll have a pint.

    Arthur finally finishes with the paper.

Arthur Aye, that's a good article is that, Harry. Champion!

Bill Int it best interview's ever been printed in that newspaper ever?

Arthur I don't read it so I don't know but I liked bit about Germans, cos they *are* swine, aren't they?

Charlie They're never our friends.

Bill And never will be. I hope.

Arthur But I disagreed with bit about Hennessy hanging, didn't you? I always thought he were a nice lad, and there weren't no proper evidence agin him, were there?

Charlie No proper evidence, no.

Bill Just the word of thieves and coppers, weren't it? No actual people.

Fry, put out, notices Harry's mind is elsewhere, as everyone drinks.

Fry Anything the matter, Harry lad?

Alice comes downstairs again.

Alice Is there still no sign, Harry?

Harry and Syd exchange a look.

Harry No. (*Pause.*) There's still no sign.

Blackout.

Interval.

Act Two

SCENE SIX

A small, simple café, early dark evening, a few hours later. It's raining heavily outside the café windows as Mooney eats at a table: beefburger, chips, beans, and a mug of tea. Syd looks in through the glass door, sees Mooney, enters.

Syd You didn't take her, did ya?

Mooney I didn't what?

Syd Harry's daughter. She's gone missing. You didn't take her, did you?

Mooney Why would I do that? That mope. Take her where? Chessington Zoo to see the monkeys?

Syd Oh, good! No, good! I put two and two together and came up with all sorts, didn't I?

He sits at the table.

They said you stopped by this morning but you stormed off.

Mooney I did stop by this morning but storm off. His dreary missus was doing my fucking head in.

Syd What did you storm off for? I thought you were going to try to get a room.

Mooney I was, but I changed my mind at the last minute. And d'you know why, Syd?

Syd Why?

Mooney Because I am my own man. I do my own thing. Like Nietzsche.

66

Syd Oh.

Mooney Do you know who that is?

Syd Aye.

Mooney No you don't.

Syd I thought the plan was to get a room.

Mooney You thought the what was?

Syd The plan was.

Mooney The plan? What plan? There is no plan.

Syd There's a sort of plan.

Mooney What sort of plan is this, pray tell?

Syd Plan to take that bigshot bastard down a peg or two. Plan to scare the living daylights out of him so next time he'll think twice before shopping his mates to Prison Commissioners over one single cock joke in the heat of the moment.

Mooney That was the plan, was it? That was a great plan. I'm sitting here having a beefburger with Field Marshal Montgomery.

Syd I were there planting seeds in his mind all afternoon.

Mooney Were ya? Seeds?

Syd But then I heard about his Shirley going missing, so I got out of there sharpish. I got worried. I thought, Christ, he hasn't gone *that* far, has he?

Mooney What seeds were these?

Syd Seeds about the Hennessy business, and all the stuff you said about dates coinciding . . .

Mooney Dates *do* coincide . . .

Syd And me being visited by a creepy-looking fella . . . *menacing*-looking fella . . .

Mooney *Menacing*, not creepy.

Syd Aye.

Mooney Did you say menacing or creepy?

Syd Menacing.

Mooney (*pause*) I don't look creepy, do I?

Syd No. You? No. *Menacing*.

Mooney Yes, I was gonna say. (*Pause.*) And how did it all go with your seeds? Did they all bloom into little northern rhododendrons?

Syd Well. it went champion, for a time, he seemed shook. But I thought he were shook about creepy lad . . . *menacing* lad renting his room out, not menacing lad taking his Shirley away. That's *too* menacing, int it?

Mooney That stupid mope, she's probably gone off to visit her mate in that mental home and not told no one.

Syd You're not allowed visit mental homes, are ya?

Mooney I don't believe so. I've never tried. I'm sure I will one day.

Syd What, when you finally go bonkers?

Mooney (*pause*) No, when my mum does.

Syd Oh. Is she troubled, your mam?

Mooney I wouldn't say she's troubled but she's never been fucking normal. But you can get away with anything when you've the cash, can't you? Money talks, I've always found.

Syd Aye. I dunno. I never had none. Especially after Harry bloody Wade stuck his oar in. Any road, aye, it were going grand although he weren't really going for it proper at the outset, he's got such a thick bloody hide, don't he? He thinks he's never done a thing wrong in his life. So I sort of had to start sort of embellishing things a bit towards the end.

Mooney Embellishing, did you say?

Syd Aye. Adding to the details of, like.

Mooney I know what embellishing is.

Syd Y'know, I said, y'know, about the Lowestoft girl that had been attacked, I said that the menacing lad had sort of . . . shown us photos of her. On the beach, there.

Mooney Say that again? I mean . . . Say that again?

Syd Photos, aye, I probably went too far with that, didn't I? I thought that after. I thought, that goes a bit further than 'He's been menacing', don't it? Or 'That's vague hearsay'. That goes more like 'He's shown me actual evidence that connects him to a specific crime', doesn't it?

Mooney It does, doesn't it, Syd?

Syd Yes. As I say, I realised that after.

Mooney (*pause*) I feel like I'm the accomplice of a former chimpanzee. (*Pause.*) Well, you'll just have to go back and tell him you were mistaken, won't you?

Syd Well, I can't do that, can I? Then *I'd* be in trouble.

Mooney Hmm. Let me think. (*Pause.*) I think you've fucked everything up, now, haven't you? Let me think. Let me work this out and see if you *have* fucked everything up or not. Hang on . . .

Syd Well, I . . .

Mooney No, don't talk. I am thinking.

Syd Yes. (*Pause.*) I thought things might get tricky after I heard their silly daughter went and got lost, cos they dote on that girl.

Mooney She didn't get lost, did she? I've got her in a garage in Formby. Now let me think. Let me plan this out.

Syd You've what, Peter? (*Pause.*) You've what, Peter? (*Pause.*) Formby?

Mooney Yes, it's by the seaside. Now, if I walk into that pub right now, what will their attitude toward me be? Not, as planned, that I am a *vaguely* menacing individual who turned up saying some *vaguely* menacing things at *vaguely* the same time their daughter went missing and who by all means requires a vague eye being kept on, *no*. That I was *definitely* involved in an attack on a girl a year ago, carried out on the anniversary of the hanging of a man who was *definitely* hanged by a man who's daughter has just *definitely* gone missing. A daughter who I was *definitely* seen having a chat with this morning. This morning *definitely* being the second anniversary of the hanging of said first man. (*Pause.*) There's a few too many 'definitelys' in there, ain't there, Syd? There's nothing 'vaguely menacing' in there, is there?

Syd There's nothing v- vaguely menacing about having a girl in a garage in Formby either, is there?!

Mooney No, there isn't, is there? That's quite specific, isn't it, 'a girl in a garage in Formby'. That's quite *specifically* menacing.

Syd You've made me quite sick, now. I were worrying about this all the way over.

Mooney Were ya? All the way over? *And* in the rain.

Syd And now it's true. What's she doing there? What have you done to her?

Mooney Nothing really, she's just hanging about. No, literally, I stood her on her tiptoes on a family-size box of Weetabix with a noose round her neck. I tried Rice Krispies first, but they kept bursting. It's in their nature, isn't it, Rice Krispies. Too airy. Weetabix are more sturdy, although I do hope she doesn't sneeze. (*Checks his watch.*) I won't tell you exactly where the garage is, eh, Syd? Keep things on a need-to-know basis, eh?

Syd What else did you do to her?

Mooney Like I said, need-to-know basis. Don't worry, I may have my quirks but I'm not an animal. Or am I? One for the courts to discuss. (*Pause.*) Talking of which, or not talking of which, I met Hennessy once, d'you know? I never told you that, did I? When I picked you out. You met him once and I met him once . . .

Syd *I* picked *you* out . . . How'd you pick me out?

Mooney My meeting was more pleasant than your meeting, of course. He survived my meeting. I met him outside a B&B in Walthamstow. I was going out, he was coming in. He was coming in with quite an ugly tart and I remember thinking at the time, 'James, if you're going to the trouble of paying for a tart, there's absolutely no need to go for an ugly one. You do have a say in the matter. We're not in Scotland.' (*Pause.*) He tried to sell me an Aston Martin for sixty quid. Well, I knew it wasn't his, he had a pyjamas top on instead of a shirt. I thought, 'That car's not yours, mate, you're not even dressed the part.' Pyjamas top, selling a sports car. Attention to detail was not one of Hennessy's strong points. Still, you don't deserve to hang for it, do you? (*Pause.*) Or do you? (*Pause.*) Poor old Hennessy. I feel quite sorry for him. He couldn't rape mud.

Syd You've made me sick to my stomach, you have.

Mooney You do look a little pale. But that's your problem, isn't it, your poor tummy. That's nothing to do with me.

Syd It *is* to do with you. It's all your fault.

Mooney It is my fault, isn't it? I'd have to admit that. If there's one thing you can say about me, if there's one thing I've learned in the years since Hennessy went down, it's that, these days, I do know when to hold my hand up and say fair enough, that was my fault, that was. (*Pause.*) Although you're still partially culpable with this Shirley one, aren't ya?

Syd What am I going to do now? I don't know what to do.

Mooney That's your look-out, isn't it? More importantly, what am *I* going to do now? Do I walk back into the pub as if I own the place, just for the laugh? Do I go back to the garage, have another tickle? Or do I say balls to all this and go back to London and civilisation? It's at times like this I ask myself 'What would Hennessy do?' And the answer is always the same: 'Something stupid that would get myself executed, so don't do that, do the opposite.' (*Pause.*) Hmm. Pub? Garage? Home? Choices, choices, choices.

He puts on his coat and goes to the door.

I'll see you, Syd.

Syd I'll go to the police!

Mooney You can't, can you, Syd? *Culpable.* Unfortunately.

He opens the door. It's still pouring down, thundering too. He pops open his umbrella.

I'm glad I brought my umbrella! I'm always thinking ahead, me!

72

Mooney exits, and Syd watches him through the
windows, as lightning flashes and thunder rumbles.
Syd slowly turns back to the room.

Blackout.

SCENE SEVEN

The pub, same evening, still storming and raining
heavily. The pub isn't open yet, so only a few lights on
near Alice and Clegg, sitting at a table, looking through
photos of Shirley. Harry hovers behind them.

Alice Well, this were the *most* recent of her, but it might
be too blurry.

Clegg It *is* a bit blurry, int it?

Alice I think she were jumping up to catch something.
I can't see what.

Harry It's a cake.

Alice It *is* a cake. Why was our Shirley jumping up to
catch a cake?

Clegg Do you have anything closer to her face, Mrs
Wade? Perhaps a school one?

Alice I do! I've one in her uniform at St Margaret's,
(*tearfully*) although she were only eleven.

Harry Don't cry, lass. There's nowt wrong yet, is there?

Alice No, I know . . .

Harry She's only been gone a few hours, really.

Alice It's just sad looking at her when she were so young
and sweet-looking, int it?

Harry She's still young and sweet-looking, int she?

Alice She is, aye. If she comes back safe I won't care how much she eats.

Harry Or mopes.

Alice Or mopes. He said she were mopey yesterday, to her face.

Harry I didn't.

Alice You did.

Harry Well so did you, if we're pointing fingers.

Alice I didn't. I waited till she was gone.

Clegg I think I'll go with the school one, over the jumping up one.

Alice Aye, go for that one. She's more still in that one.

Harry Jumping up for a cake. You're supposed to jump up for a ball.

Alice Well, it doesn't matter what you jump up for, does it, as long as you come home safe! She could jump up for a banana as far as I'd care!

Harry I know, love. I know.

Clegg puts the photo and his stuff away.

Clegg Well I'll try to get this in for the final editions, Mr Wade, but failing that, first thing in morning.

Harry Thanks, lad, and thanks again for the article this morning, it were right good, weren't it?

Clegg I'm glad you liked it. I wasn't sure if you would.

Harry Of course I liked it. It were forthright. Opinions. No cocking about. *Me*!

Clegg Mr Pierrepoint hasn't been round to punch you in the nose, has he?

74

Harry That queer? I'd like to see poof try.

Alice Albert Pierrepoint were always lovely to me . . .

Harry Oh, give over . . .

Clegg Did *you* like the interview, Mrs Wade?

Alice We're here for our Shirley, aren't we? Not interviews.

Clegg Aye. Aye.

She drinks her gin as he fixes to leave.

Harry I'll walk you to door, lad, and you go easy on that gin!

They walk to the door.

Alice (*quietly*) It's *my* gin.

Harry (*to Clegg*) It'll be alright, won't it? Our Shirley?

Clegg Oh, of course, Harry, I've no doubt. I mean, she's not even missing technically, is she? She's probably just gone off on her own for a bit.

Harry She's probably just gone off in a mood, int she? Something her mam said.

Clegg Aye. Anyways, I'll get these in. I'll see ya.

Harry I'll see ya, lad, aye. Mind that rain.

He unlocks the door, lets Clegg out, then locks it again and comes back to Alice. He puts a sad hand on her shoulder, and she pats it, almost crying.

Alice D'you remember when she were five, Harry . . .?

Harry No, no. Don't start that.

Alice Start what?

Harry That 'Remember when she were five' shite, like she's dead or summat . . .

Alice I wasn't . . .

Harry She int dead, she's fine, she's just gone off moping like a fool, and she'll get a hiding when she gets back, so let's go with that, alright? Smiles on, gruff exterior, let's get this pub open. Right?

Alice Oh, can't we stay closed for one night, Harry?

Harry Course we can't. It'd be like something's wrong, 'stay closed'. And nowt's wrong, is it?

Alice Something's wrong. I know it in my heart.

Harry (*pause*) Aye, the cheery angel voice of the hopeful fucking bright side. Don't say owt to this crowd, any road, we don't need everybody knowing our business, do we?

Alice (*quietly*) I don't care who knows.

Harry Oh stone me . . . (*Quietly.*) No wonder she turned out a mope with you about.

He goes and opens the doors, turns up the lights, etc., as Alice finishes her drink and goes behind the bar. Heavy rain outside as Harry turns the outside light on.

Fix yourself up, Alice. Put that gin away.

Alice powders her teary face a bit as Charlie, Bill and Arthur enter, one umbrella between them, which bounces rain on to them as they bang through the door.

Charlie Mind that bloody umbrella, Bill, you pisshead! You got water all down me bloody neck now. Oh sorry, Alice, I didn't see you there, I were saying to Bill.

Alice Hello, lads!

Harry Pints all round, is it?

Charlie It is!

Bill We're parched!

Arthur Despite the rain!

Bill By, Harry, there int a soul in town int read that article of yours! There was a coloured lad int bookies, well, I don't usually talk to him. He comes up, he says, you know that Harry Wade fella, don't ya? I said so what if I do, what's it to do with you? He says, let me shake your hand, that were the best article I've ever seen printed in that newspaper. I said, well thank you, I agree!

Harry That's great, Bill. That's great.

Bill Aye, it's . . . vicariously, int it? (*Pause.*) He's often in there. I don't mind him, I just don't talk to him, like, y'know? He's black.

Harry Aye.

Harry and Alice pull pints through an uncomfortable silence.

Alice Did you have any winners, Bill?

Bill No. (*Pause.*) Bastards. (*Pause.*) I had a fourth. Miss Pixie.

Alice And you don't get nowt for a fourth, do ya?

Bill Well, it depends on the size of the field, don't it? You do get summat if field's big enough.

Harry How big were field for your fourth?

Bill Well, aye, five.

Harry Five?!

The others laugh.

You didn't come fourth, you just didn't come last! Five!

Arthur What were it?

Charlie Just horseracing stuff you wouldn't get.

Arthur Oh.

Harry How much did you have on it?

Bill Well, aye . . . tuppence.

Harry Tuppence?! The last of the big bloody spenders! Tuppence! Miss bloody Pixie! Fourth out of five!

Bill Well I don't have a lot of money to spend on horses, do I?

Harry I can see you don't!

Bill Cos I spend it all bloody in here, don't I?

Harry I know you do!

Bill Because I'm a bloody alcoholic, aren't I? I know that! You don't have to bloody say it!

    An embarrassed silence.

Harry What are you talking about, Bill? You're not alcoholic. You just like a drink, you.

Alice You just like a drink, Bill, aye.

Charlie Aye.

Arthur What were it?

Charlie Bill's saying he's alcoholic. We're saying, 'You're not alcoholic. You just like a drink, like,' y' know?

Arthur But he is alcoholic, Bill, int he?

Charlie He's not Arthur, shush. If *he's* alcoholic, we all are!

    Harry looks at them like they all are.

Bill Aye. Well . . . I were fine, drink-wise, weren't I? Before me wife left me . . .

Harry Oh Bill, look, I don't want to hear any of this tonight, alright, I've me own problems. Alright? And, no, you *weren't* fine before your wife left you, that's *why* she left you, your drinking. So just have another pint and stop worrying, lad. Life's too short to be listening to your problems. Give lad a drink ont' house. Christ!

Charlie On what?! Ont' house?!

Bill Oh, thanks, Harry! That's right nice, I'll have a Scotch.

Harry You'll have a half and be glad.

Bill I'll have a half, Alice.

Arthur A drink on the house from Harry Wade! Blimey, who's died?!

Alice almost start to cry but manages not to.

Harry No one's died. (*Pause.*) Fool.

Door bangs open, and Inspector Fry comes in, collar up against the rain, newspaper over his head, soaked.

Fry Ay-yi-yi!

Charlie How do, Inspector.

Harry and Alice look at him, both hopefully and worried, but he shakes his head, and they visibly sag. He hangs his overcoat up and comes over.

Fry No, we checked the mental home in Burnley, they said no one came calling round there, so that's that ruled out, unfortunately . . .

Harry (*interrupting*) Shall we talk about this upstairs, Inspector?

Fry Eh? Why? I were going to have a pint.

Harry Oh.

Alice pours his pint.

Fry And we've issued a description of the southern lad throughout county, so . . .

Harry (*interrupting*) Yeah, just I think it'd be nicer to talk about this upstairs, don't you? So why don't we do that, George, we'll talk about this upstairs.

Fry But what does it matter, Harry? The more people know, the better . . .

Harry Upstairs, I says, and I won't say it again. I'll lead the way with your pint. Alright?! Good! Follow me. Upstairs.

He has taken the pint from Alice and leads the way upstairs. Fry, irritated, follows, leaving the cronies dying for the gossip from Alice, who cleans the bar with a rag.

Bill Everything alright, Alice?

Alice Oh aye, aye. (*Cleaning.*) Can't complain, y'know?

Arthur (*pause*) How's your Shirley, she alright?

Alice nods a while, then shakes her head.

Alice No, no, she's been sort of missing since morning. We were hoping she might've tried to go to Burnley to try to see her mate Phyllis in that home there . . .

Arthur Aye, no, Inspector just said she didn't, didn't he? No.

Alice Aye. No. So we're a bit worried, now. Well, we were worried before. We're more worried now. Well, *I* am.

Bill Don't be worried, Alice. She's a good head on her, int she, your Shirley? She's very smart and she's very kind.

Alice She is, int she, Bill?

Bill Aye. I'm sure she'll be fine.

Arthur You *hope* she'll be fine. You're not *sure* she'll be fine, cos you don't know.

Bill The odds are, Arthur, she'll be fine. Alright?

Arthur Aye. (*Pause.*) Although Inspector seemed worried.

Charlie Inspector seemed fine, Arthur. He just has one of them faces.

Arthur (*pause*) Harry seemed worried. He don't have one of them faces. He's usually upbeat.

Alice Aye, but we're all a bit worried, int we?

Arthur Aye. You said.

Alice 'Worry', it's a good thing, int it, 'worry'? It means you love her, don't it, 'worry'? It means that you care.

Arthur Aye, I suppose. I'm off for a wee, anyways, I were holding it.

He heads off to the toilet, leaving the others to just look at each other.

Bill By heck, Charlie lad . . .

Charlie I know . . .

Bill Sometimes I just don't know where he's going with these things, do you? I know he's half deaf but Christ. 'Inspector seemed worried.'

Alice He don't mean nowt, do he?

Bill That's the thing, Alice, he don't mean nowt at all. Then you come away from a night with him thinking the world's just bloody ended.

Alice My world would end, if it were true.

Charlie Don't think that way, Alice love. She'll come walking through that door any . . .

Door bangs open, and in comes Mooney, shaking off his umbrella.

Mooney Cor, what a miserable rainy day! What is it about the north of England and rain? Now, I know what you're going to say, Mrs Wade . . . Hello, lads . . . Now I know what you're going to say, Mrs Wade, you're going to say 'What's that git doing back here when he stormed off so rude this morning, effing and blinding about my husband and all the people he hung?' Let alone my giving you all that rubbish about how sneaky you were phoning up my references when why shouldn't you phone up my references? It's *your* room, isn't it? It's *your* phone. Why shouldn't you phone up my references? And why shouldn't you do it behind my back? You don't have a phone down here, do you? I realised that afterwards. So why shouldn't you phone up my references behind my back? Also, maybe you wanted to ask my references some tricky questions it'd be best me not hearing, and why shouldn't you? Why shouldn't you ask my references some tricky questions it'd be best me not hearing? Y'know, things like 'Do I pay up on time? Do I play music loud? Am I normal?' Things any landlady would require answering, let alone the mother of a pretty young girl. So I've brought my references back for you, here they are, and I just wanted to say that I am still interested in the room if you're still interested in me. I'll have a pint while you think about it, and whatever the boys are having, cos I've come into a little bit of pocket money since we last chatted.

Charlie Oh, that's right kind of ya, lad . . .

Bill Aye, ta . . .

Alice No . . . No . . .

Mooney No what, Mrs Wade? You're just saying 'No', aren't you?

Alice I'll have to . . . my husband's upstairs . . .

Mooney Is he? Upstairs?

Alice Aye . . .

Mooney Good for him!

Alice I'll have to talk to my husband.

Mooney But he's upstairs, isn't he? We're down here. Why don't you talk to him after you get the pints? Why don't you do that? We're parched!

She starts pulling the pints, very flustered.

And the customer is always right, of course. I wasn't right this morning, though, was I? I was well wrong. My language was the least of it. Coupled with that was my attitude. It *was* early, though, I'm not at my best in the mornings. Are you?

Charlie Our friend Arthur's int' loo, but I'm sure he'd be happy to have a pint with ya too, Mr . . .?

Mooney Alright. You're pushing it a little bit with that, aren't you, but alright. A pint for Arthur too. Is the room still free then, Mrs Wade, did you say?

Alice No. Not to you.

Mooney Not to me? You haven't forgiven me, have you? I can see that now. I can see it in your face. In your lovely old face. My language *was* reprehensible, I know, but I'm not like that when you get to know me. I'm quite mild.

Alice Your pints are there. I've to go and see my husband now.

Mooney But you haven't poured Arthur's pint yet, have you? He'll be seething when he comes back from the loo to find himself left out. Pour Arthur's pint.

Alice does so.

Charlie Arthur don't seethe. He's too deaf to.

Mooney Well, that's nothing to do with me, is it? And why don't you get yourself a nice big gin, Alice? So we can let bygones be bygones. I'm sure it's a lovely room. The room was never the issue.

Alice I don't want a gin. Not from you.

Bill What's going on, Alice?

Alice What's going on . . .?

Arthur returns, doing up his fly and rubbing his hands on his trousers.

Arthur I remember this lad. He's new!

Mooney And I remember you, Arthur. Cheers!

Arthur You're the Babycham man.

Mooney (*pause*) No, I'm not the Babycham man. I had all this yesterday! I've never touched Babycham in my life.

Arthur No, you *bring* the Babycham.

Mooney I don't do anything with the Babycham! You've got the wrong man!

Charlie It's a different man brings the Babycham, Arthur. The Babycham man brings the Babycham.

Arthur Who are you, then?

Mooney I'm just a bloke, aren't I? I'm hopefully the future lodger. If things pan out. That's all I am.

Charlie He's bought you a pint, any road, Arthur lad. So just be nice to him.

Alice You don't have to be nice to him. He's got something to do with our Shirley going missing. I know that. I'm not daft.

Bill Eh?

During Mooney's next speech, Harry and Fry start coming down the stairs and see him.

Mooney I know what's happened. Oh, here he is now, you don't have to go and get him now, do you? Save your old legs going upstairs. I know what's happened. Someone's been chatting to my old friend Syd Armfield, haven't they? Someone's been chatting . . . Hello, Inspector, hello Mr Wade. Someone's been chatting to my old assistant-hangman friend Syd Armfield, haven't they?

Harry and Fry are stunned by Mooney's presence, and the cronies obviously all know something's up but aren't sure what.

Harry What the hell's this?

Alice He just came in and he started chatting, Harry, and I were just about to fetch you . . .

Mooney Yes, Alice is right. I just came to apologise for how rude I was this morning. She had every right to phone up my references. I said that to myself after I stormed off, I said to myself, 'Why shouldn't she phone up my references? Why shouldn't she?' What the hell else are you supposed to do with references? You could write to them, like in the olden days, but that'd take ages, wouldn't it, defeat the object.

Fry has circled round the back of him, between Mooney and the entrance.

Mooney I can see you.

Harry Alright, alright, enough of this. Where's our Shirley?

Fry Keep calm, Harry. We'll be fine now. It'll all be fine now.

Mooney Your daughter Shirley? The mopey one? She not about?

Alice I were just about to come get ya, Harry . . .

Harry Shut up.

Mooney Don't talk to your wife like that, old man! I know you're the hangman and everything, but fucking hell! Y'know? Fuck me.

Fry What's your name?

Mooney Me? My name? Mooney. What's your name?

Fry Fry. Chief Inspector Fry.

Mooney Nice name. Big shot. Small Fry. You decide.

Harry Enjoying that pint, are ya?

Mooney I'll say yes to that question to save an argument, but if I'm being completely honest, Harry, and I don't know if it's a northern thing but this particular pint is a little bit pissy. It's a little bit . . . how shall I put this? It has a little bit the hint of piss about it. Maybe it's your pipes, I don't know how that sort of thing works. How's *your* pint, Arthur?

Arthur It's alright, mine.

Mooney It's alright, is it?

Arthur Bit warm.

Mooney Bit warm, but not pissy. Good combo!

Fry Where've you been since twelve this afternoon, Mr Mooney?

Mooney Good question and by the looks on your faces, and by the whad-ya-call hanging in the air, the tension or

86

whatever . . . I am thinking Mr Syd Armfield, former assistant hangman and sometime vague pervert, has been chatting with you. Would that be correct, Harry?

Harry It's Mr Wade to you.

Mooney Oh, play the game, old man. It's a revelation, isn't it, that Syd and I are on friendly terms?

Harry No. He told me you came to see him two day ago.

Mooney I know, and I showed him a bunch of photos about the blah blah Lowestoft blah blah. All made up, of course. No, I'm talking about half an hour ago. Yeah, I just had dinner with Syd half an hour ago. You didn't know that, did you? Burger and chips I had, and I'm not being funny, it's not just the drink up north that's piss-fucking-rotten. How can anybody muck up burger and chips? I mean, how? It's burger and chips! Even the beans were rank. How can you muck up baked beans? You only have to open the can, surely? That's all *I* do. I don't know what people around here do.

Fry Not from around these parts, are ya, Mr Mooney?

Mooney We've established I'm not, Inspector. Keep up.

Fry Where are you from then?

Mooney Boy, you're a good policeman! Isn't he, Bill? You owe me a drink, Bill, I haven't forgotten. I'm from down south, me, aren't I? Norfolk area. Hennessy territory. That direction.

Fry Lowestoft way, would it be?

Mooney No, never been to Lowestoft.

Fry Oh no? How comes?

Mooney It's all just riff-raff, Lowestoft.

Fry How would you know if you've never been?

Mooney I've never been to Africa, but I know it's full of monkeys.

Arthur (*pause*) And spiders.

Mooney (*beat*) And spiders. Big ones. Triantulars.

Fry So Lowestoft is riff-raff, but you're not riff-raff?

Mooney Well, riff-raff is in the eye of the beholder, isn't it? It depends who's judging, doesn't it? If you and Harry were judging, no way am I the riff-raff, compared to you and Harry. Because you're from the north. So it depends who's judging, doesn't it? If Søren Kierkegaard were judging then, yes, compared to Søren, prøbably I *am* the riff-raff. If Søren was feeling particularly judgmental that day. Or normal judgmental, I'm not sure what he was like. Have you read much Kierkegaard? Has that question ever been asked in Oldham? I haven't read much Kierkegaard, I haven't read any, I choose not to. I just like his funny name. A lot of philosophers have funny names, don't they? How'd that happen? (*Pause.*) Talking of riff-raff, my old friend Syd Armfield would be the king of the riff-raff. Of course he's not my friend, is he? That's patently clear, I hardly know the man, but neither is he the innocent northern bumble-fuck he purports to be. In fact, if it's true that your daughter's gone missing, and by your face and your manner I'm assuming it *is* true, well, I wouldn't start pointing fingers at a bloke who, although vaguely menacing, *has* walked right into your pub for a drink and a chat, and a bag of peanuts, actually, which I forgot before, could I have a bag of peanuts, Alice?

Harry indicates to Alice – no peanuts.

Alice No, you can't have any peanuts.

Mooney *I'd* point *my* finger, or, if not point my finger, because it's rude to point, I'd do an 'indicate with my

88

eyebrows towards' the individual who *hasn't* walked into your pub, and who *does* have a criminal conviction for pervy things. I don't, you see? I don't have a criminal conviction for anything. You, copper, I forgot your name already, you can look that up. Peter Aloysius Mooney. No convictions for nothing. That doesn't mean I haven't done nothing, of course. It just means if I do do things, I'm quite good at doing them, and I get away with doing them. (*Pause.*) That, or, y'know, it's a made-up name.

Harry May I have the floor please, Mr Mooney? You have been chatting for quite some time.

Mooney It's your floor, Harry, you can do what you want with it.

Thwack! Harry smacks Mooney across the back of the head with the same billyclub he used on Hennessy. Mooney goes down on one knee.

Fry Jesus Christ, Harry . . .!

Harry Where is she? I already asked you civil.

Mooney I didn't expect this kind of behaviour from a hangman. I expected a cultured debate.

Thwack! Harry clubs Mooney again. Mooney goes down on both knees, bleeding now.

Mooney Oh for God's sake, man . . .

Fry Harry!

Harry Shut it!

Mooney There's only one word for what you're being now. Riff-raff! Well, two words, isn't it, it's hyphenated . . .

Harry Pass me the barrel rope, Alice.

Alice Aye.

Alice grabs a lengthy coil of rope and passes it, as Fry grabs Harry.

Fry We're taking him down station, Harry, and questioning him there.

Harry Take your hands off me. I'm quite calm. I'm getting him a chair.

Slowly, Fry does so. Harry sits the dizzy, bleeding Mooney on a chair downstage right, below a beam in the ceiling with a curtain hanging along it.

Bill? Go lock that door. You? One more time. Where is she?

He forms a simple noose with the barrel rope as Bill goes to the door.

Mooney I never thought I'd say this but, boy, I could do with a Babycham right now . . .

Harry twists the noose tight around Mooney's neck, choking him. Just as he's doing so the door creaks open and Syd comes in, rain-soaked, and his jaw drops on seeing the strangling Mooney.

Harry Sydney. Perfect timing . . .

Syd No, I were just popping me head in . . .

Harry Come o'er here. Bill, lock that door . . .

Bill locks the door and turns the lights low as Syd comes over.

Syd No, I can't stay . . .

Fry Harry!

Harry You, shut it, you've been useless all day. Alice, a towel for Syd and pints for everyone, ont' house.

Arthur (*happily*) By heck, lads!

Harry Syd? This fella says you and him are old mates and you ate together tonight, that right?

Syd Of course it ain't right, Harry! This is the fella I were telling you about, came to see me with them photos.

Mooney struggles against the rope, trying to kick or punch at Syd.

Harry Get us something to strap his arms, Alice. What have we?

Alice We've an arm strap!

Harry Perfect!

Alice passes the arm strap to Harry . . .

Arthur What is it?

Charlie An arm strap.

Arthur Perfect!

. . . and Harry gets Mooney's arms strapped behind him.

Mooney Don't do that, I've got a bad wrist.

Harry You'll have worse than a bad wrist when this is over.

Mooney Will I? *You* will.

Harry Where's our Shirley?! Eh?!

Mooney Ask him, he knows.

Syd I don't know. How would I know? You know.

Mooney You know what'd be great right now, Syd? A family-size box of Weetabix, d'you know where I could get one?

Harry Lad's a bloody loon! Get him up ont' chair!

He throws the rope up over the ceiling beam as Bill, Syd and Harry stand Mooney up on the chair under it.

Mooney Oh you're having a laugh, aren't ya? I mean it was funny before but this is getting silly now.

Harry pulls the rope tight over the beam and around Mooney's neck, so he's on tiptoes.

Charlie Blimey!

Fry Harry! For Christ's sake, man!

Harry Calm down, George! So it's alright to do this down cop shop but int alright down pub, is that right?

Fry When have I ever done this down cop shop?!

Harry Well, maybe you should start, you might solve summat. Where's our Shirley?

Mooney (*strangled*) I can't speak . . .

Harry and Bill release him slightly.

Harry Where's our Shirley?

Mooney The name rings a bell . . .

Harry pulls the rope, with Bill's help, hanging the struggling Mooney six inches off the chair. He gasps and stuggles and starts going red. With Bill taking the strain, Harry quietly walks up to him.

Harry You'll have two more chances. The third time I'll take the chair away and that'll be that, and we'll go out and look for her ourselves. Alright? Now, is she somewhere in Oldham still?

He gestures to Bill, who lowers him back to his tiptoes on the chair.

Mooney Can't breathe . . .

Harry You can breathe. You only need a little air, really, it's surprising how little you need. It's your vertebrae you want to be worried about. Now, is she somewhere in Oldham, still?

Syd Ask him if he's got her out somewhere like near the seaside, like out Formby way or somewhere.

It's only really Inspector Fry whom this strikes as very strange.

Harry Do you have her out near the seaside or somewhere . . .?

Syd Like out Formby way.

Harry (*beat*) Like out Formby way?

Syd Like maybe in a garage?

Mooney You're a bunch of bloody nincompoops!

Harry and Bill hang him again. Charlie and Arthur sip their pints.

Fry Right, that is it, Harry. I'm calling round a squad car.

Harry keeps watching the struggling Mooney a few seconds more.

Harry (*to Fry*) I were always harder than you. I tolerate you, but you're nowt. So shut your fucking face. Alright?

Arthur I heard that one!

Harry gestures to lower Mooney again, and his feet touch the chair, but he seems to be in a bad way, gasping for air.

Harry It's your last chance, lad. I'm talking quietly now cos I know you'll hear me anyway. Cos my voice is all you've got now, int it? It's all you've got to hang on to.

It might be the last voice you ever hear. Don't let it be, lad. Don't let it be. (*Pause.*) Where is she?

Mooney She's . . . (*Gasping.*) She's . . .

Harry Aye?

Mooney She's up shit creek . . . and I don't think she's got a paddle . . . which is very dangerous . . . cos she was never a lightweight girl, was she?

Mooney and Harry look at each other a moment, then Harry helps Bill hang him again. His legs thrash a bit this time so Harry ties them together with a rope. Just then there's a very loud and determined banging at the door.

Male Voice Open bloody up!

Everybody looks at each other as the banging continues.

Harry (*whispered*) Lower him back ont' chair!

They lower Mooney so his feet touch the chair again, but the rope gets stuck there.

Bill It's bloody stuck!

Harry Well, stick summat in his gob to stop him yapping! And cover him up!

Syd sticks a rag in Mooney's mouth, and they pull the curtain along the beam so that only the chair he's standing on can be seen from the entrance side of the stage. The banging at the door is even more heated.

Male Voice Open bloody up, it's pissing down out here, and I know you're there, I can see you moving!

Alice I know who that is.

Harry (*glumly*) I bloody do too.

Alice opens the door and in walks a well-dressed man of Harry's age, shaking off a wet umbrella.

Alice Oh, hello, Mr Pierrepoint. What brings you to Oldham?

Pierrepoint Alice, I don't mean to be rude but it's your husband my business is with tonight.

Harry Hello, Albert. It's Albert Pierrepoint, everybody!

Pierrepoint Don't hello Albert Pierrepoint everybody me, ya bloody bastard, and don't introduce us to your cronies neither, cos if they drink in your pub they must be the dregs of the bloody earth. Look at them, they *are* the dregs of the bloody earth! Now I were handed today a certain newspaper opinion piece that were printed in a rag called the *Oldham Gazette* . . .

Harry It's not an opinion piece, is it, it's an interview. 'An opinion piece' . . .

Pierrepoint I don't care what it bloody is!

Harry And it int a rag, it's a good newspaper, int it, lads? The best in Oldham!

Charlie (*same time*) I suppose.

Bill (*same time*) It's one of them, aye.

Arthur (*same time*) I don't really read it.

Alice Can I offer you a drink, Albert?

Pierrepoint No, Alice, I'm not stopping. I just came in to say me piece.

Harry Well say your piece, then go then. We're busy.

Pierrepoint slowly walks up to Harry, who gets a little scared.

Pierrepoint What did you just say?

Harry Didn't say nowt, Albert. Just . . . we were in the middle of summat.

Pierrepoint What were you in the middle of? Being a whiny, insecure, dicky-bow wearing fuckpig who was never any good at his fucking job?

Harry No. Other things. (*Pause.*) Weren't we, Inspector? Other things.

Pierrepoint Oh, hello, Inspector Fry . . .

Fry Hello, Albert . . .

Pierrepoint You're one of his cronies now too, are ya?

Fry I'm not. And I said he shouldn't've done that interview, neither.

Harry Ah, here, George . . .!

Pierrepoint Alright, I'll let you off hook. It's this toerag I'm after. Does the word 'sacrosanct' mean anything to you, Wade?

Harry Oh 'sacrosanct sacrosanct sacrosanct'! It's always 'sacrosanct' when it suits you knobs! It's 'spilling the beans' when I do it! It's running away with meself when I do it! Well, two words, Pierrepoint. Jealous. Git. Just cos you're not hangman no more and I am.

Pierrepoint You're not hangman no more neither, Harry.

Harry I wouldn't be so sure of that, Albert. Now say your piece and get going cos my friends and I are very busy people.

Pierrepoint moves over towards the curtain area, where Syd and the chair and Mooney are.

Pierrepoint Oh, hello, Syd, I didn't see ya there.

Syd Hello, Albert.

Pierrepoint Standing in corners like a mouse, is it?

Syd (*sighs*) I s'pose.

Pierrepoint Pull us up that chair will ya, Syd. This might take a minute and me back's bad.

Syd looks at the chair that Mooney's on, looks at Harry, doesn't know what to do . . .

Syd This chair?!

Pierrepoint Aye, any chair.

. . . until he's saved by Bill dragging over another chair from the background.

Bill Here, Mr Pierrepoint, this one's a cushion on it.

Pierrepoint Ta, lad.

All breathe a metaphorical sigh of relief as Pierrepoint puts a foot upon his chair, hat in hand, and starts to speak.

Often when I think of you, Harry Wade –

Harry Oh, bloody hell . . .

Pierrepoint – my mind harks back to one of our first jobs together. That anarchist lad we did in Pentonville in the forties, d'you remember? French lad, big mop o' hair?

Harry Vaguely.

Pierrepoint I remember him. I remember him clearly. I remember looking in on him through spyhole throughout night, that night that was to be his last. He couldn't communicate with his warders, of course, he was French, but at each tolling of the church bell throughout night, his final night on Earth, he'd count off on his fingers the hour they tolled: if it were two he'd count two, if it were four he'd count four, but then he'd keep on counting, counting on up to eight, the hour of his impending doom. Then he'd point to himself, then he'd point skywards, then he'd smile. And with each passing hour he'd do same. Count the hour. Count to eight. Point to himself. Point to Heaven. Smile. (*Pause.*) He'd killed a man robbing a jeweller's in Clerkenwell, a stupid crime, the usual, yet I thought then, and I think now, that there were more integrity in the finger that that doomed Frenchman pointed to a Heaven he didn't believe in than you, Harry Wade, had in the entirety of your shitty, fat, nondescript, Oldham publican's fucking life. Not only is your pub shite, you were a shite hangman an' all!

Harry My pub's not shite, my pub's great, and I were a better hangman than you on top of it, and everyone agrees, don't ya, lads . . .?

Pierrepoint With your bow ties and your bowler hat and your fat fucking grin. I'd pity the murderer who'd wind up with you at door, I would! Throughout years, I would! 'Oh great, I'm off to die and me hangman's a fat fucking circus clown!' I'm surprised none of them complained!

Harry I had no complaints, I can tell you that!

Pierrepoint I'm surprised none of them asked for me!

Syd looks at Harry.

Harry Why would they ask for you? Like you're bloody famous or summat! Cos you're not!

Arthur Well, he is.

Harry Shut up!

Arthur He's most famous one.

Pierrepoint Fucking bow ties! You were always late! Always complaining about the food! You never did *any* Germans . . .!

Harry I were busy that week! I were busy that week! It were Grand National Week!

Pierrepoint It were more than a week, Wade. It were a war. You were a coward then, you're a coward now. A bluff, arrogant, stupid coward. I always felt sorry for Alice for having to put up with ya.

Harry Aye, because you always bloody fancied her, didn't ya?!

Pierrepoint (*pause*) No. No, I never fancied her. I'm sorry, Alice, but your Harry's brought this up. I always thought she were a pleasant woman, but I never thought she were pretty or owt. I were always happy with my Anne, you see? I were never that type of man. You were. 'Grand National Week'.

Alice and Harry exchange a look.

Harry Alright, I may've never hung any Nazis, but at least my hair doesn't smell! Your hair does! It stinks!

Pierrepoint My hair doesn't smell.

Harry It does. It always did. It smells of death. Anyone'd tell ya if you bothered to ask them.

Just then the chair that Mooney was standing on topples over behind Pierrepoint, meaning the gagged Mooney is quietly strangling to death behind the curtain. Syd is standing near the chair, looking sheepish. Pierrepoint slowly goes over, picks up the chair, and leans in towards Syd.

Pierrepoint Smell my hair.

Syd smells Pierrepoint's hair. Pierrepoint drags the chair over to the cronies and Alice, leans in again.

Smell my hair.

They do so. He drags the chair past Harry and over to Fry.

Smell my hair.

Fry does so. Pierrepoint places the chair to one side.

What does my hair smell of?

Fry Brylcreem.

Arthur (*same time*) Brylcreem.

Bill (*same time*) Brylcreem.

Charlie (*same time*) Brylcreem.

Alice Brylcreem.

Harry I weren't allowed smell it, were I?!

Pierrepoint goes over to Harry, who smells it.

Stale Brylcreem, aye.

Pierrepoint Don't smell of death though, do it, Harry? (*Pause.*) Don't smell of death though, do it, Harry?

Harry (*mumbled*) No. Stale Brylcreem.

Pierrepoint If there's a smell of death around here, int off me. (*To Harry.*) No more interviews. Alright? And no more talking behind my back. Alright?

Harry Alright, Albert, alright. I just lost run of meself, didn't I? It won't happen again. You can go now.

Pierrepoint Alright. No need to rush me, is there? I only just arrived.

He slowly puts on his raincoat, doing up all seven buttons . . .

I had to get two buses.

He puts on his hat, shakes off his umbrella.

I'll see ya, Alice love. Sorry it weren't under happier circumstances.

Alice See ya, Albert. I never had any problem with ya. It were him.

Harry Oh, go if you're going!

Pierrepoint And give my love to your Shirley. She must be right big by now.

Alice nods tearfully. Albert goes out through the door. The rain has stopped, and his shadow lingers a moment through the frosted glass, then is gone. All the men stay frozen for a moment, then rush as one to the curtain, chair in hand, to save Mooney . . . but it's clear to us all from the way he's hanging there that he's dead.

Syd Oh Jesus Christ, oh Jesus . . . !

Fry Oh bloody hell . . .

They lower or cut him down into Harry and Syd's arms and lay him down on the floor, undoing the noose and gag. Fry checks for a pulse as Alice and Syd stand there, horrified. Fry slowly stands back up.

Nope. Dead.

He pulls the curtain down, covers Mooney's body with it, and blesses himself.

Syd Oh heck. Oh bloody hell. What the hell do we do now?

Fry What we do now is, you start talking, Syd. You know something about all this that we don't, don't ya?

Syd I don't . . .

Fry You know something about Formby, you know something about garages, and you know something about Shirley going missing . . .

Syd I don't. I don't know nowt!

Harry starts slowly approaching Syd and Fry.

Fry Then we'll do this down cop shop, shall we?

Syd Cop shop? I'm not going down cop shop. Why don't we just chat pleasant while we drive around somewhere? Somewhere seasidey, maybe . . . y'know, like, I don't know, *Formby* or somewheres . . . and see if we happen to pass any garages or owt . . . and see if we can hear, y'know, anybody talking loud or . . . shouting or, y'know . . . choking, or owt. O- o- on the off-chance, like?

Harry You aren't being serious . . .

Alice He int being serious . . .

Syd I don't know nowt, Harry! I swear I don't . . .!

Just then, the door bangs open and in comes Shirley, dressed up pretty and talking at full pelt.

Shirley Alright, I *know*! I *know* you're going to be bloody mad and I *know* it's been hours and I *know* I should've bloody rung, but I don't bloody care, do I?! I were waiting for me new fella, Peter, yes, Peter, and I don't care that you don't like him cos I *do* like him, or I *did* like him until he never came back, so more fool me for falling for somebody in one stupid day, just because he drove me to Burnley, which was closed, and to the seaside, which was rainy, and to his place where he was nice to me for ages, and didn't call me a mope once, and more fool me for believing him when he said he thought I weren't his type at first but he changed his mind when he got to see the real me, and more fool me for not realising he only wanted the one thing, but maybe I only wanted the one thing too, you never think of that, do ya, that I've got feelings too, and more fool me for waiting in a train station with tramps for four hours when I knew he wasn't coming after the first two, I'm not stupid, am

I? But then the rain started again and I thought I may as well keep waiting as walk home in that, I'd get drenched. So then two hours turned into four, didn't they, and I'm bloody here now, aren't I, so can't you just tell me off tomorrow, Mam, I'm starved?!

Alice goes over to her, puts a gentle hand to her face.

Alice Aye. I'll get your tea now, love, and there's a pudding I made special earlier, we could have that for afters.

Shirley A pudding? Oh yum, what kind?

Alice Blancmange, your fave.

Shirley Oh Mam, blancmange, yum, that's brilliant. Are you not going to tell me off then?

Alice No, love.

Shirley Are you not mad I've been out with a fella all day?

Alice I don't care, do I? I just love ya, don't I?

Harry *I'm* mad you've been out with a fella all day.

Alice Aye, well, we don't care about you, do we?

Shirley No, we don't care about you, do we, Mam?

Alice (*looking at him disdainfully*) 'Grand National Week'.

The ladies start to head off upstairs together, arm in arm.

Shirley It int nowt, is it, mam?

Alice What int nowt, love?

Shirley Sex and that. I thought it'd be all angels and Elvis but it's not, is it, it's just fumbling and sad and then he doesn't even love ya a half-hour after.

Alice That's about the size of it, aye.

Shirley Oh Mam! I know it's wrong but I think I still love him! D'you think he still likes me?

Alice looks back at Mooney's corpse on the floor.

Alice Why don't we just have a chat about it over our tea?

They exit.

Harry (*pause*) Well just don't let her eat all that pudding on her own! There's other people in this house besides her!

Syd (*pause*) Well, I'll be off then.

Harry You bloody won't! You'll be helping us dump this fella with these lads.

Bill With which lads? With us lads?

Charlie I'm not helping dump nowt, Wade.

Harry Oh, 'Wade' now, is it?

Bill (*to Syd and Harry*) Aye, why don't yous two do it? You can take his arms, Harry, and you can look at his cock, Syd.

The cronies laugh, as they start to head out.

Charlie That were a good one, Bill!

Arthur Cock!

Syd I did that *once*!

Bill We'll see ya, Inspector Fry.

Charlie See ya, Inspector. See ya, Harry.

Arthur I'm glad your Shirley's back safe, anyway, Harry. That's the main thing, int it?

Harry It is, lad. Aye, it is.

Arthur It would've been awful if she was dead.

Harry It would, Arthur. You're right, lad. I'll see you lads tomorrow.

Charlie (*same time*) See ya, Harry!

Bill (*same time*) See ya, Harry!

Arthur (*same time*) See ya probably tomorrow then, I suppose.

The cronies exit . . .

Bill Oh good, rain's stopped. Looks like it's going to be a right nice evening.

. . . leaving Harry, Fry and Syd alone to look at each other a moment. Harry points at the body.

Harry You've a car, don't you, George?

Fry No.

Harry You *do* have a car.

Fry No, you're wrong, lad. I'm *nowt*, aren't I? I'm *tolerated*, aren't I? Nowt and tolerated don't have a car, do they?

Harry You do, you've a Ford Allegra.

Fry Good luck, lads. I weren't here. Alright?

He exits.

Harry He's always been a lazy fucking bastard. (*Pause.*) And his wife's a pig.

They look at the body a moment.

Syd Mooney's got his Morris Minor outside. We could put him in that, drive him int' canal.

Harry We could! (*Pause.*) Will you do it, Syd? I think I pulled summat hanging him.

Syd (*sighing*) Aye, alright.

He kneels down and starts going through Mooney's front trouser pockets.

Harry (*disgusted*) What are ya doing?!

Syd Car keys.

Harry Oh! Good! I thought . . . No. *Good!*

Syd finds keys, rattling them happily as he stands back up.

I still haven't forgiven you for whatever your part in all this was. I just can't figure out what your part was.

Syd Well, let's leave it at that then, shall we, let bygones be bygones. We're friends again now, aren't we, Harry?

Harry We're not friends, no. I'm just glad Shirley's not dead, so I've moved on. (*Pause.*) I'd've hung meself if Shirley was dead. I would.

Syd 'Hanged'. You'd've 'hanged' yourself if Shirley was dead.

Harry glares at him, then smiles.

Harry You're less of a knob than you used to be. I don't know how.

Syd Thanks, Harry. You too.

Harry gives him another look. Pause. Harry points down at the corpse.

Harry So *did* he have owt to do with Hennessy killing? I can't work it out.

Syd I don't know. I thought not, before, but I don't know what to think now. He were a very strange man, whatever he were.

Harry He int strange now. He int nowt now.

Syd No. He's just dead now.

Harry Aye, Syd. Always the first with the boring bloody obvious, that was another reason I grew to dislike ya. It weren't just cocks. (*Pause.*) Although cocks were the biggy.

Syd Aye, well, we've moved on from all that now, haven't we, Harry?

Harry Aye, Syd. We have.

They shake hands over the corpse. Pause.

Well, it were definitely *either* him or Hennessy, weren't it? So, y'know, close enough.

Syd Aye, it were more than likely one of them, weren't it? So . . .

Harry Aye. Or both of them, perhaps. Somehow.

Syd (*pause*) Or neither.

Harry Aye, or neither. (*Pause.*) I suppose that's just the way it goes, int it? With justice. (*Pause.*) Ah well. You get arms, I'll get legs.

Syd Like int' old days!

Harry Aye, like int' old days! (*Pause.*) I'll miss it. (*Pause.*) I will. (*Pause.*) I'll miss it.

Syd nods. They look at the corpse.

Blackout.

End.